I AIN'T GOT
TIME TO BLEED

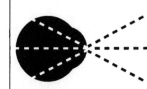

This Large Print Book carries the
Seal of Approval of N.A.V.H.

REWORKING THE BODY POLITIC
FROM THE BOTTOM UP

I AIN'T GOT TIME TO BLEED

JESSE VENTURA

Thorndike Press • Thorndike, Maine

Published in 1999 by arrangement with Random House, Inc.

Thorndike Large Print ® Basic Series.

The tree indicium is a trademark of Thorndike Press.

The text of this Large Print edition is unabridged.
Other aspects of the book may vary from the original edition.

Set in 16 pt. Plantin by Minnie B. Raven.

Printed in the United States on permanent paper.

Library of Congress Cataloging-in-Publication Data

Ventura, Jesse.
    I ain't got time to bleed : reworking the body politic from
the bottom up / Jesse Ventura.
      p. cm.
    ISBN 0-7862-2214-X (lg. print : hc : alk. paper)
    1. Ventura, Jesse. 2. Governors — Minnesota Biography.
3. Minnesota — Politics and government — 1951–
4. United States — Politics and government — 1993–
5. Large type books. I. Title.
F610.3.V46A3   1999b
977.6′053′092—dc21
  [B]   99-44121

This book is dedicated to Terry, Tyrel, Jade, Bernice, and George

ACKNOWLEDGMENTS

Thanks to everyone who made this book possible and my life what it is and will be. My wife of twenty-four years, Teresa; my son, Tyrel; my daughter, Jade; my brother Jan; my mom, Bernice Lenz Janos; my father, George Janos; my South Side buddies Jerry, Kevin, Lynn, Harley, Charlie Wannabe, and all the others; Steve Nelson and all my Navy underwater demolition SEAL teammates; Barry Bloom and Mike Braverman; Ken and Vincent Atchity and the AEI team, especially Julie Ann Mooney; Bruce Tracy and everyone else at Villard; and all the people alive or dead I may have forgotten.

I would also like to thank Steve Bosacker and all of my current government staff and commissioners; my campaign staff and volunteers; all those who voted for me; and Shirley Chase, Alan Eidsness, and David Olsen, the three best lawyers in the world.

Thank you to all I include and those I have undoubtedly omitted.

CONTENTS

Acknowledgments

CHAPTER 1

THE AMERICAN DREAM

I didn't need this job. I ran for governor to find out if the American dream still exists in anyone's heart other than mine. I'm happy to say that it does. I'm living proof that the myths aren't true. The candidate with the most money isn't always the one who wins. You don't have to be a career politician to serve in public office. You don't have to be well connected or propped up by special-interest groups. You don't even have to be a Democrat or a Republican. You can stand on your own two feet and speak your mind, because if people like where you're coming from, they will vote you in. The will of the people is still the most powerful force in our government. We can put whomever we choose into office, simply by exercising that will.

We're a nation of bootstrappers. We're visionaries. And we're not afraid to turn our visions into reality. That's the great thing about Americans — the word *can't* isn't part of our vocabulary. We've always been a can-do people. And we still are, despite all the negative things we hear about how corrupt our government has become, and despite the fact that we've become too reliant on that same government for things it has no business providing. We might have lost sight of it a little bit, but we are still the keepers of the American dream.

How else could a guy like me have become the governor of Minnesota? Look at me: I'm no career politician — I'm a six-foot-four, 250-pound ex–Navy SEAL, pro wrestler, radio personality, and film actor. I only got into politics in the first place because I have a pretty noticeable habit of speaking my mind. But I guess a good bit of what I had to say must have made sense to people, because they elected me twice.

This book is mostly about me, about where I stand, and about where I came from. But what's happening in Minnesota right now is far bigger than me. History is being made. Like many other people across the nation, Minnesotans are fed up with the good-old-boy network that cares more about keeping itself well ensconced than it does about carrying out the voters' wishes. In 1998's gubernatorial race, I gave them an alternative.

I'm a Minneapolis native with working-class roots. My collar's indelibly blue. I belong to the private sector, and that's where I'm returning the minute my term as governor is over. I stand for the common man because I am him. That's one reason the people of Minnesota elected me: I know where they're coming from because I came from the same place.

They also voted for me, I think, because I'm not easy to ignore. I'm big, I'm loud, and I'm not afraid to say what I think. But I also got a powerful set of ethics from my parents, some serious hard-core discipline from the Navy SEALs, and some decent people skills from my careers as a professional wrestler, film actor, and radio personality. And I can talk to people without talking down to them.

But if I had to pick one reason Minnesotans voted for me, I would have to say that it is because I tell the truth. I stand tall and speak freely, even when it isn't politically expedient to do so. That, above all, is what I think Minnesotans voted for: honesty.

This book has two purposes: first, to tell you where I stand — and why — on the issues that affect us all. Anybody who offers themselves for public office owes you that; and second, to tell you the story of what made me who I am. I'm an ordinary guy who went for his dreams and made them happen. The only things I've ever been handed are extraordinary guidance and life-long friendship, without which I could never have achieved all that I have. But I'm no golden child. I've had basically the same opportunities as most of you. And if a guy like me can become the governor, so could you. That's the way American government is supposed to work.

Unfortunately, there's an idea out there that's very destructive to the American electoral system. It's the idea that you have to cast your vote for whoever's most likely to win, because otherwise you're wasting your vote. That is simply not true. There is no such thing as a wasted vote.

Voting is not supposed to be just a popularity contest. It's not like betting on a horse race. It's our responsibility when we vote to vote for the ideas we would like to see become public policy. We have to choose our candidates by the things they stand for, not by their ratings in the polls. When we bow to the pressure of the polls, we get exactly the phenomenon we're complaining about now: career politicians who will say anything to get your vote and who don't stand for anything except what the latest poll tells them to support. Yet somehow, that's become the standard. But it doesn't have to be that way.

I understand why so many people don't vote anymore, and I sympathize with them. It can seem like a waste of time when the only candidates you see in the news are cookie-cutter copies of the ones you saw in the last election and the election before that. But these days you have to look beyond what the media tells you to think and make up your own mind about the issues. Your choices aren't limited to the party favorites who have the money and the influence to get themselves into the limelight. You can vote for anybody you want. My stand on voting is that if you don't cast your vote, you forfeit your right to whine about the government.

When I announced that I was running for governor, everybody said I couldn't win. They said my campaign was an exercise in futility. The media thought I was a joke. My opponents pretended I didn't exist. But on November 3, 1998, the people of Minnesota came out in droves and made it happen. This election had the largest voter turnout (in years without a presidential election) in Minnesota's history and almost the largest in the country's history. We shocked the world. We wasted the system with "wasted" votes.

My Democratic opponent, Attorney General Hubert H. "Skip" Humphrey III, called our victory a "wake-up call of the first order." Even my Republican opponent, Saint Paul Mayor Norm Coleman, said that we ignited a spark, even though he said he didn't have any idea what that spark was. They knew I was popular, but neither of them had any idea how I won.

How did I do it? With a secret weapon that the other two candidates didn't have: The people who put me in office were overwhelmingly people who had never participated in the system before, and a huge number of these new voters were college-age people.

The bottom line is that my opponents were boring. They were the same old brand of career politicians, the kind that comes out of the woodwork every four years, spouts the same old rhetoric about the same issues, and then disappears. People don't bother to come to the polls anymore because they don't see the point. The candidates are virtually indistinguishable from each other. Minnesotans might not have been quite sure what they were getting when they voted for me, but one thing they knew for sure: It wouldn't be business as usual!

There's a brand-new generation in Minnesota that has just come into the electoral system. They saw this election as an opportunity to be heard. They've infused Minnesota politics with new blood. And as long as we do what we have to do to keep this new generation involved, we're going to turn this system around.

My victory is important for another reason. I'm the first member of the Reform Party to win a statewide office. There's been talk recently that the Reform Party has had it. People have been saying that we're going to go the way of most other third parties: We'll show up and bark just loud enough to get the two traditional parties back in line a little, then we'll quietly disappear. But our government needs more than just a face-lift — it needs a major overhaul. The Reform Party's work is far from over. In fact, it's barely begun.

We have to build this party from the bottom up. It must be a grassroots organization, or else it's meaningless. And if you look at it that way, then no election is insignificant. No win for the party is too small. A government that is truly by the people has to be grassroots at its foundation. It has to come from the bottom up.

Think of the alternative. If the party's controlled from the top, then whose hands is it in? Career politicians. The comfortably ensconced people who are many levels removed from the working people of this country. The fact that our nation's government is controlled by people like that is at the heart of every complaint I hear about our government today.

Standard operating procedure in our political system today is that everyone's owned, either by one of the two parties or by special-interest groups. Career politicians are bought and sold. And that's how I'm different: No one owns me. I come with no strings attached. All the lobbyists in Minnesota are running scared right now because suddenly the rules of the game have changed. They have no leverage with me. They have no in.

One of the first things I did during the transition period between the election and the inauguration was to bring in thirteen citizens from across the state. These were people who were either first-time voters or who hadn't voted in five consecutive elections. I asked each of them a question: Now that you've come into the system, how do we keep you involved?

Their answers were very clear, very honest. They said, It's the same story every four years. Whenever an election's coming up, all the politicians come out and give you the same song and dance about the same issues, all the way up until they get elected. Then you don't hear any more from them until it's time for them to get elected again. We're tired of it. If you want to keep us involved, don't tell us what you think we want to hear, tell us the truth.

There's a great need in our government right now for honesty. All you have to do is look at what's going on in Washington these days to see that. I've always told the truth, because I believe it's the right thing to do. But coming from the private sector gives me a credibility that career politicians don't have. I have no hidden agenda. I don't need to tell you what you want to hear so I can get reelected. I have a very successful life waiting for me outside of politics; I don't need to get reelected.

Anyone who's known me through the years, in any of my various careers, will tell you that I speak my mind. I'm incorrigible when it comes to that. You might not always like what you hear, but you're gonna hear it anyway. I call it like I see it; I tell the truth. And if I don't know something, I'll say so. Then I'll try to find the answer.

I decided to run for governor because I got mad. In 1997, the State of Minnesota had a budget surplus of more than four billion dollars. The voters wanted that surplus returned to them because, in their opinion, they'd been overcharged. But Minnesota legislators chose to ignore the wishes of the people and instead dreamed up all kinds of pork-barrel projects to make themselves look good when reelection time came. Some of that surplus money was bonded to pay for high-profile projects that the people didn't want. As a result, our children are going to have to assume the payments on the out-of-date convention centers and sports facilities these politicians built to help themselves get reelected. Is that how we show our children we care for them? Is that the kind of public servants the voters really want?

I also saw that a lot of people had no voice in decisions affecting their taxes. For example, there's a group called the Metropolitan Council that can levy taxes in a seven-county area that makes up the Twin Cities, even though the council seats aren't filled by elections. Nowhere else in the state is there this extra layer of government. Another example is people who own lakeshore property. They are also highly taxed but receive very few municipal services and have no say in policy matters. In my book, these are both cases of taxation without representation.

I want to make government more directly

accountable to the people. If I'd run for governor and lost because no one was interested in or cared about what I want to do, that would have been fine with me. It's their choice. But I wasn't going to be weeded out because the system said I couldn't win.

My campaign was anything but run-of-the-mill. My opponents were in suits. I was wearing jeans and a Minnesota Timberwolves jacket, and my campaign slogan was "Retaliate in '98." Since so many people were convinced I didn't have a chance, early on in the race the thought of voting for me was considered pointless but fun. Garrison Keillor even said voting for me was like throwing toilet paper in the trees to piss off Dad. I became the candidate of choice for the rebellious. But I went out and made myself available to people. I listened. And I learned.

Unlike my opponents, not a penny of my campaign money came from special-interest groups. Instead, my supporters relied on Minnesota's Political Campaign Refund program, which allowed them to donate fifty dollars each to my campaign, and then get a fifty-dollar refund from the state after the election. I spent $600,000 on my campaign; my opponents together spent close to $13 million.

I knew that in order for the campaign to work, everyone in the state needed to know that Jesse Ventura was a candidate for governor. Many people are not on the Internet. Many people don't read newspapers. But nearly everyone watches TV, so that's where I focused my campaign. I got on TV and promised the people that there would be no big-money power brokers behind the scenes, yanking their governor's chain. I promised I'd be there to serve the people, not the special interests. And I promised to be honest with them.

A lot of people laughed at the idea of this big, beefy feather-boa-wearing ex–pro wrestler and film actor as the head of state. OK, so maybe it's funny. But there are precedents. Other entertainers have successfully gone into politics: Ronald Reagan. Senator Fred Thompson. Clint Eastwood. Sonny Bono. Even Gopher from *The Love Boat*, Fred Grandy. I'll let you in on a secret about being an entertainer: It's all about communicating, about being able to see things from a bunch of different perspectives. There's a lot about entertainment that translates directly to the kind of public relations that you have to do in politics. When you're serving in a public office, you have to be able to communicate extremely well. It didn't bother me all that much that people laughed. To tell the truth, it bothered me more when they stopped laughing after the election.

It's strange how before this victory, nobody took me seriously. Now, suddenly, everyone's lost their sense of humor. Yes, I now have a heavy responsibility, which I take very seriously. But I'm still the same person I always was. It reminds me of Voltaire's quote about God being "a comedian playing before an audience that can't laugh." That applies to me, too — not to put myself on God's level, but people take me as far more serious than I am. I don't know where our sense of humor has gone in this country. I'm finding out that when I talk to the media, a lot of the time I have to throw up my hands and say, "That's a JOKE!"

Politics is not my life. I have a career in radio and another career in film. I have a wife who is the sweetest person in the world and two kids who are growing up into terrific, well-rounded people. I don't need or want to spend the rest of my life in politics. When I'm finished with my term as governor, I'm going back to the life that's waiting for me in the private sector. For one thing, it pays better. And for another, none of the other careers I've had in my life has kept me trapped in my own home and under

21

surveillance twenty-four hours a day. I'm accustomed to answering only to myself and my family. Now I have to answer to the entire state of Minnesota. But I'm taking on this responsibility, willingly and voluntarily, because I have a vision for how to make things better. And as a citizen of the greatest democracy in the world, I have a duty to do my small part.

This is all new to me, and I feel a little like the Rodney Dangerfield character in *Back to School*. But I'll adapt. I'll do what needs to be done. The responsibility doesn't scare me. I've been through SEAL training. I've faced death and lived to tell about it. Nothing that happens in the next four years can possibly be as tough as that.

You can rest assured that I have plans for the next four years. I'm here to affect policy as much as I can. But no matter how the next four years go, I've challenged the status quo and won. I've restored people's confidence in our political system. I've awakened their hope. My victory is part of a much bigger picture. It's a wake-up call. It's the beginning of a political revolution.

CHAPTER 2

SOUND BODY, SOUND MIND

Where I'm Coming From

I am not a career politician. I'm not a Democrat. I'm not a Republican. I'm a working man with commonsense ideas and goals. I describe myself politically as fiscally conservative and socially moderate-to-liberal.

We need to keep a permanently tight rein on government spending. I believe working people should keep as much of their money as possible, and I believe they should have a more direct say in how it's spent. But I don't believe we need the government's help as much as some think we do. That belief sets me apart from the Democrats, since their way of dealing with everything is to tax and spend.

I also believe that government has no business telling us how we should live our lives. I think our lifestyle choices should be left up to us. What we do in our private lives is none of the government's business. That position rules out the Republican Party for me. As the cliché says, "I don't want Democrats in the boardroom, and I don't want Republicans in the bedroom."

So I stand before you as an advocate of minimal government interference and of minimal public reliance on government, which in anybody's book ought to spell lower taxes. And that pretty much keeps me out of both parties.

That's the way I want it. Neither of the two parties is truly representing the people anymore. They're at opposite extremes, with about 70 percent of us in the middle. That needs to change, and that's why I'm a member of the Reform Party.

Right now, too much of the business of the government is focused on keeping itself in business. A lot of its programs are set up so that when they are working the way they're supposed to, they spend more tax dollars and cause the government to bloat even further. Unless we do something, the cancer will just keep spreading. At this point, maybe all we can do is apply chemotherapy to keep it from growing any further. Our government's growth is becoming harder and harder to control.

What's worse, as time goes on, we're getting more and more into the habit of looking to the government to solve our problems. I believe the American people are capable of getting along just fine with a whole lot less help from the government. Common sense, fiscally and socially, is more helpful than a dozen new laws. I think if the average person thought about it that way, he or she would tell you they'd rather keep more of their tax money and use it to solve their problems on their own!

Yet the cancer continues to spread. We have far more laws on the books, for example, than we really need to do the job. Just because you're a legislator doesn't mean your job is to create more laws for people to live by! During my transition period, I went into Secretary of State Joan Growe's office. One entire wall of her office was filled with books — volume after volume of Minnesota's laws. And the court decisions interpreting those laws fill an entire library. Now, you've heard that ignorance is no excuse for breaking the law. So every citizen has to know all those laws? It would take years!

There are professionals whose job it is to be experts in the law. They train for the same amount of time as medical doctors, and they still have to lug around these huge, ponderous law books, because even they can't keep it all in their heads! If we're going to hold average citizens responsible for knowing the laws, don't you think we'd better make sure the laws are knowable?

I believe in the K.I.S.S. rule: Keep It Simple, Stupid. In many cases, the laws we already have on the books would work just fine; they'd do the job if we would just become more serious about enforcing them. A new law is not always a better law.

Government programs suffer from the same kind of unchecked, cancerous bloat. The number of special interests out there is constantly growing. Everybody has a wish list. Everybody has a cause. If we indulged everybody's wish list, we'd be paying 60 to 70 percent of our income to the government! We need to set priorities. We have to learn when to say no. Nobody has a right to government money just because they have a cause. There are a lot of good causes out there, but they can't possibly all be served by government. I think in their heart of hearts, most people understand that the government cannot function efficiently when it becomes a charity organization. The Constitution guarantees us our rights to life, liberty, and the pursuit of happiness. That's all. It doesn't guarantee our right to charity.

The government is not a parent. We can't expect the government to always be there, ready to bail us out. When we make decisions in life, we have to be willing to live with the consequences. We can't expect the government to help us get back on our feet every time we make a bad decision. We have to accept responsibility for the decisions we make. That goes for education, career moves, family planning, the whole nine yards. Certainly, there should be some kind of government safety net; government has a role in helping us out in genuine crises, but a line has to be drawn somewhere. We can't look to government every time we make a decision that causes us to tighten our belts a few notches.

We've gotten in a bad habit of overlegislating. I believe in the American people's ability to govern themselves. I believe that if government would just get out of the way and allow them to lead their lives as they choose, they will succeed. Government only needs to be there to support them in their efforts.

Remember that government doesn't earn one single dollar it spends. In order for you to get money from the government, that money must first be taken from somebody else. It's amazing to me how often people lose sight of this. It's not fair for a person who wanted to go to college but not work for it, or who decided to have kids when they weren't financially ready, or who made a poor business decision, to take money from someone else. In many cases, the person they're taking it from only has money to give because they made sounder decisions. Do we want to penalize people for leading their lives responsibly? Do we want to send people the message that it doesn't matter if they are financially responsible, since the government will always be there to force other people to bail them out?

If public service is going to work as it should, public servants have to know who the public they're serving really is. To do that they must first have spent time building a life the way we working people have, or our concerns will never be real to them. You can't have a government of the people, by the people, and for the people if the people who operate the government spend the vast majority of their adult lives, or at least of their careers, inside an isolated and, in a sense, artificial world. They're making decisions that profoundly affect the average American citizen, yet they have no idea what life for the average American citizen is like! They've never been there, or it's been so long they can't remember.

You've heard the old saying that power corrupts and absolute power corrupts absolutely? That's what comes into play when public servants make a career out of what they do: They eventually have to shift their focus from serving the public to serving their careers. It's not a career if you don't get reelected! So that becomes your objective: winning the election, staying in the game. Raising money. To hell with the "public service"!

On the other hand, when somebody who isn't a career politician takes office, everyone understands that it's temporary. They'll serve one or two terms, then they'll be out. They have a life and a career somewhere else. Odds are, they themselves will be affected by the legislation they pass or the programs they implement during their term. They probably sought office because they felt strongly enough about one issue or several issues to want to do something about them. This is the mind-set we want in our public servants.

Where I Stand on the Issues

Government Reform

If you haven't got my point yet, I'm saying that we need to take control of our government out of the hands of career politicians and special-interest groups and put it back into the hands of the people. As it now stands, we're overly dependent on a system that seldom has our best interests at heart.

The two major political parties wield far too much power. Their control over the political process is deeply entrenched and embedded in the system, and it's carefully orchestrated to keep nonparty candidates out and to keep the two parties in control. But that's not how it's supposed to be. Government is supposed to represent us, not the two parties.

We desperately need to reform government so that we can reclaim more of the decision-making power in our lives, as well as keep more of the money that we earn. We're a capitalist society. Government's role is not to baby-sit us. It's to provide the basic infrastructure and essential public services that will best facilitate our individual and collective prosperity and freedom. Beyond that, it has no business interfering in our lives.

Term Limits

Term limits are the most effective means of keeping career politicians out of the system. After an individual serves the prescribed term, he or she gets a one-way ticket back to the private sector and makes way for someone else from the private sector to step forward. That dynamic link to the world of the common citizen is vital in keeping government on track.

Campaign Reform

Our campaign laws desperately need an overhaul. Do you know how difficult it is for anyone coming directly from the private sector to get into office? There are all kinds of roadblocks and catch-22s and technicalities set up to keep the two traditional parties in power. The will of the people can hardly even be heard through the current maze of regulation!

We need to set up our campaign system so that who gets to run is not a matter of how much money they have or whether they belong to a party. Campaigns have become far too expensive, and the average candidate ends up selling out to special-interest groups in order to obtain the funding to run.

When candidates accept special-interest or political-action-committee money, they are indebted to the group that is funding them. In effect, they've been bought. It's legalized bribery. Campaigns should be funded only by the people, from small, indi-

31

vidual donations, so that only those individuals that the people truly want will participate.

Legal Reform

Our legal system has gotten sadly off track. Justice cannot be just if it's swayed by wealth or celebrity status. There is hardly a more infamous event in our recent legal history than the O. J. Simpson trial. It was a travesty of justice that has left permanent scars on the judicial system, just as I have permanent scars on my forehead from wrestling.

All the evidence points to O.J.'s guilt. There's not a shred of evidence that points to anyone else. Yet Judge Ito caused the prosecution's case to be lost. He allowed testimony and evidence into that trial that should never be allowed. You can't put the cops on trial when there is no evidence they did anything illegal in connection with an arrest or investigation; if we allow that, what criminal case could ever be successfully tried? Everyone has things in their background that they're not proud of, and if you allow that background to be scrutinized closely enough, you can weaken anyone's credibility.

What is worse, Johnnie Cochran cheated.

It was reported that he went into O.J.'s house before the jurors toured it, took down pictures from the wall, and hung up pictures of Dr. Martin Luther King and other prominent black leaders, to make it appear as though O.J. was somehow still concerned about the black community. He wasn't. I was invited to go on Cochran's talk show, but I refused, because he willingly violated the law and manipulated his craft as a lawyer to let a double murderer walk free.

That trial taught me that if you have enough celebrity status in this country, you can get away with anything — including murder. We're celebrity worshipers. Any average person would have been convicted within a week. The memory of that case has left a permanent stain on our country's history. The only positive thing we could possibly do now is to let that memory stand as an example of what's wrong with our judicial system as we look for ways to fix it.

Taxes

In a capitalist society, problems are best solved by lowering taxes, not by making government larger. The best-case scenario is for government to empower the people by letting them keep as much of their money as possible, then support them in the decisions they make. Government works less efficiently when it begins to grow out of control and takes on more and more of the responsibilities that belong to the citizens.

A case in point is the shortage of affordable housing we have in Minneapolis. We have two choices: We can create yet another government program, pass more laws, provide more subsidies, and enact more restrictions — with the result that we'll end up raising taxes. Or we can lower taxes so that we make it more attractive for private-sector builders to build in those areas. *It must be made profitable for the private sector.* You can't just keep flushing more and more money into more and more government programs. If we allow the government to swell and fatten and bloat, who is going to foot the bill for it all? Look in the mirror.

Consumption Tax Versus Income Tax

I'd like to see the income tax replaced by a national consumption tax. Instead of being taxed for making money, individuals would be taxed only when they make a purchase. They could control their taxation rate by controlling their spending habits. They would no longer be penalized for working and saving their money, and it would allow them to get their money before the government does.

With a national consumption tax, each person will decide how much of their money the government is going to get. And if the people are in control, government spending will then have to become sensitive to the economy. And because tax collections will not increase when times turn bad, it would force government to live within its means. After all, the rest of us have to.

Refunds for Budget Surpluses

As governor, I have to create the budget. And I believe that whenever we have a surplus of revenue above what is needed to run the government, that money should be returned to the taxpayer. The utility companies do that, why can't government? The Democrats always argue that as long as there's tax money left over, we can always find good, worthy programs to spend it on. That's true. But there's another way to handle that: It's called "No!" If there are programs that the taxpayers want to give money to, then let's put it in the budget. But we can't be looking for excuses to spend money just because we have it to spend. The bottom line is, if there's money left over on June 30, after the budget is balanced and the fiscal year is over, it should go back to the people who paid it. Plain and simple.

The K.I.S.S. rule applies to how we send it back, too. The citizens don't have time to watchdog the government; they're busy working and raising families and trying to survive. We have to set up a refund mechanism that runs itself smoothly and efficiently. People should be able to trust that every other June 30 (we have a biannual budget in Minnesota), when we balance the budget, anything that's left over will automatically come back to them. We as a people shouldn't expect anything less.

Property Tax Reform

You shouldn't be taxed because your neighbor's property goes up in value, and you shouldn't be taxed for improving your own property. We've got to simplify it, make it fair, and make certain that people are not driven off their land whenever developers move into a neighborhood.

Education

I can understand why some parents are tempted to write off public schools as a loss and send their kids to private schools. But I think that the parents who do that are losing sight of the bigger picture. We can make our neighborhood schools places to be proud of only if we're willing to invest ourselves in them. No amount of tax money can replace parental involvement.

I believe strongly that government should be encouraging parents to get involved in public schools, instead of giving them vouchers or tax credits so that they can send their kids to private schools. A recent study showed that about 72 percent of the parents surveyed would rather see their public schools improved than receive vouchers to send their kids to private schools.

I went to Minnesota public schools from kindergarten straight through to high-school graduation, and so did my son. My daughter will do the same. I think we should view our public schools as a good system that's in need of reform, rather than as a broken-down system that we should avoid. There's still far more baby than bathwater here, and I would like to see the public schools succeed. What we need to do is examine the system closely, figure out where the problems are, see what solutions to those problems have worked elsewhere, and apply them. But we have abundant evidence that it doesn't help public schools to simply throw more money at them or to keep endlessly lengthening the school year. Obviously, if something isn't working, making it more costly and making more of it just makes for a bigger problem!

There are pragmatic, commonsense steps we can take to improve the quality of the education our kids receive in public schools. The following are the fifteen steps for improving public education that Lieutenant Governor Mae Schunk and I developed during the campaign and posted on our website:

IMPROVING PUBLIC EDUCATION

1. Improve student literacy by expecting all children to read by the end of first grade.
2. Help students develop a firm foundation of learning skills by reducing primary class sizes, grades K–3.
3. Improve math and science achievement through problem solving in real-life learning experiences.
4. Encourage and enlist greater parent participation in school-improvement efforts and in decision making.
5. Become a community of partners in learning: create a strong sense of respon-

sibility and accountability for teachers, students, and parents; provide a variety of opportunities for parents to learn and be involved in their children's education throughout the year.

6. Encourage more school-community partnerships to provide volunteer tutoring, mentorships, internships, and school-to-work programs.

7. Support and take part in school and community initiatives to prevent acts of violence.

8. Encourage all junior-high-school students to take a class about parenting and family responsibility.

9. Provide quality time for professional staff development to improve curriculum instruction.

10. Provide a curriculum that reflects cultural diversity.

11. Wire every classroom to the Internet and provide staff development for training, effective curriculum suggestions, and adequate resources.

12. Provide opportunity for community-service programs that will apply as academic credit for graduation.

13. Provide more creative programs for all interested students for after school and during the summer.

14. Develop high expectations.
15. Act as if we mean it (because we do) when we say, "KIDS BELONG IN SCHOOL!"

(*Source:* The Official Jesse Ventura for Governor website: www.jesseventura.org)

Families must invest in their neighborhood public schools

One thing that's sadly lacking in our public schools these days is parental involvement. Without it, public schools can't be what we want them to be. Families have to make personal commitments to their neighborhood schools. If people truly felt deeply involved with their schools, we could turn our schools around. Parents and retirees should be encouraged to get involved in literacy tutoring, in community-service projects, in parenting classes, and in helping out with homework. That's one of the most beneficial uses I can see for the Internet: It can give parents a direct link to their children's classroom environment and can open lines of communication between parents and teachers. Education is a cooperative effort: It takes parents and teachers working together as a team.

The best way to solve most of our educational problems is to reduce class size

There's hardly a more effective way to solve the problems we face in our educational system than to reduce class size. A ratio of no more than seventeen students per teacher ensures more one-on-one contact, better classroom discipline, you name it. Study after study has consistently shown that students do better when they are in classes with fewer students.

Here in Minnesota, we have already allocated the money to reduce class size. Our problem is that there are too many loopholes in the program. The lesson to other states that will be doing the same in the future: You can't earmark the money for class-size reduction and then leave any loopholes for the legislature to spend it for anything else.

The federal government has too much control over schools

The federal government needs to leave much more of the management of public schools up to state and local governments. A rubber-stamp, "franchise" approach to schooling simply doesn't work. Students' needs vary by region; their curricula should too. What works best for one school district isn't necessarily going to work best for another. The federal government needs to loosen its control of public schools and leave more of the decision making up to local teachers and administrators, who have first-hand knowledge of what their students need.

We need to spend more on students and less on administration

Bringing the decision making closer to home will also help cut administration costs. We spend far too much of our public school funding on administration. We should be spending more of it on the students. For example, with the money we save, we can work toward getting more computers and Internet access into classrooms, as well as helping students improve their computer skills.

We've got to make sure school curricula are relevant

Each school district should be allowed to take responsibility for making sure that their curricula are relevant to their students' needs. Students are far more likely to learn when they can see a tangible connection between the lessons they are taught and real-world skills that they will need. And the people most qualified to determine the content of those lessons are the people who deal with these students on a daily basis, not a federal bureau thousands of miles away.

We should set minimum standards for all students

At the same time, though, each school district has to make sure that all students meet certain basic criteria. Every student needs to demonstrate a minimum level of competence. Every student should be able to read, for example, by the first grade.

Mainstreaming: the best odds for disabled students

There is overwhelming evidence that the best chance disabled students have for productive adult lives comes from being mainstreamed among other students. My daughter Jade is living proof of that. She has a disability, but Terry and I have made sure that she has gotten the same kinds of exposure as other kids her age. There are a few exceptions; there are students whose special needs are such that mainstreaming wouldn't work for them. But in the majority of cases, mainstreaming should be supported, encouraged, and facilitated for disabled students.

No government money for higher education

Students shouldn't simply be handed a free pass to higher education. They should have to work for it. They should at least contribute a significant amount to their tuition through part-time jobs. If they're smart enough to get in, they're smart enough to figure out a way to make it work. Part of our problem in this country is that we've lost our respect for higher education. We take it for granted because it comes so easily. We don't value the things that are handed to us the way we value something we've put a lot of sweat and sacrifice into. If we insist that students make an investment in their own educations, they'll get more out of them in the long run.

Students often approached me about state-paid tuition while I was out campaigning. After I explained to them that if the state pays their tuition now, they will pay higher taxes to pay other people's tuitions for the rest of their lives, most of them ended up agreeing with me. Skip Humphrey was promising to hand them two years of free education, and they still voted for me!

Businesses have a role to play in education, too, because they cannot compete without an educated workforce. Internships, on-the-job training, and individual grants are all win-win situations. It benefits the businesses to have better-trained employees, and it benefits the students to be better prepared to enter their trades. Government's role in this scenario should be to act only as a facilitator.

Business

Government policy should facilitate business. The more money businesses get to keep, the lower their costs will be, and the less they'll need to look to government for help. Government's role should be only to keep the playing field level, and to work hand in hand with business on issues such as employment. But beyond this, to as great an extent as possible, it should get the hell out of the way.

Businesses pay too much in taxes, just as individuals do. Businesses are overtaxed because government has taken over more functions than necessary. We need to figure out which services could be handled better by the private sector. In the hands of the private sector, unlike government, competition will keep quality high and cost low. Once we're left with only the services that government provides best, we can then figure out ways for it to perform those services as cost-effectively as possible.

Government should encourage people to start small businesses

The government should reward and encourage people who have the initiative and ingenuity to start new businesses. Above all, it shouldn't make it impossible for them to operate by hamstringing them with an extra tax burden. It's the nature of capitalism to encourage people to innovate, and government should support that.

Development

Urban sprawl and inner-city rehabilitation

There's no way we're going to be able to achieve zero-population growth. We need to understand that communities are going to continue to grow and expand. So we need to plan ahead and direct growth in a way that allows for the best use of available land and resources.

We can't just let urban growth endlessly sprawl out toward the suburbs and beyond. We'd make much better use of what we have if we revitalized our inner cities. We need to make inner-city living attractive again. We need to make it appealing to developers. If we don't do that, we'll end up with a sprawling metropolitan area that's rotting from the inside out.

I like plans that automatically help one problem while they're fixing another. With more businesses, resources, and capital flowing back into the inner cities, you get more jobs, less poverty, and lower crime.

Building on sacred lands

Even before my inauguration, folks who were protesting the rebuilding of Highway 55 through South Minneapolis on what they believed to be sacred Native American lands were trying to solicit my help. I'm not against protecting sacred lands, but if a piece of land is sacred now, wasn't it sacred thirty years ago when the housing development that will be demolished for the highway was built? Where were all the protesters then?

It makes me think that this particular issue, and others like it, are more a matter of what the popular way to react is, given the sensitivities we have in our culture right now, than they are about protecting sacred lands. We can't declare all lands sacred; we can't have somebody raise a fuss every time we want to build somewhere. For practical reasons, the line has to be drawn somewhere. Who deems what is and is not sacred? What's sacred to one is not sacred to another.

The Military

I'm against the draft. I believe we should have a professional military; it might be smaller, but it would be more effective. The draft, particularly as we saw it during the Vietnam War, is unfair. Rich kids didn't get drafted; they went to college and hid. You know who that left for Uncle Sam?

If we're going to draft at all, which we shouldn't, then we should draft women too, as long as we don't send them into combat. Now, I know that there are tough women out there who would be effective in combat. Women give birth — they're certainly able to withstand pain! There are female biathletes who could make it through SEAL training. I'm certain of that. That's not the problem.

The problem is men. There's something inherent in men that makes us want to protect women. And that would be disastrous in battle. You have to act as a unit; you can't favor some of your soldiers over the others. Can we train ourselves out of it? I don't know. If it's just a cultural thing, maybe we could over time. Human beings can override their instincts, but usually not without a good bit of effort. Besides, are we absolutely certain we want to train that protective impulse out of men?

As for our military involvement in the Middle East, I've kept an eye on what's been going on over there the last several years, and I can tell you the reason why we keep getting into scuffles with Saddam Hussein: We need him. The fact that we've kept him in power and haven't taken him out is intentional. We need a bad guy there. We need a reason to keep our military personnel on the pulse of the world's oil reserves. We put him in there — do you think we couldn't have taken him down by now if we had wanted to? And he knows it. That's why he misbehaves!

Social Issues

Crime

People are always shocked when they ask me what I plan to do about crime as governor and my answer comes back as "Nothing!" Does the issue of crime need to be addressed? You bet it does. But, just as with many other social issues, I don't think that legislation is the most effective arena in which to fight crime. We already have tons of laws on the books. Most of those laws would work more effectively if we just enforced them better.

As governor, there just isn't a lot I can do beyond that to crack down on crime. Law enforcement is really a local issue. It's the cops' job to tighten down on criminals. When I was mayor of Brooklyn Park, I rode with my cops. I'd show up at the station un-announced and take a ride in the squad car so I could see exactly what they were doing out there.

Politicians always like to say "I'm gonna fight crime!" because it sounds great and gets them votes. But when was the last time they got out there on the streets and caught somebody? What can a politician do to fight crime?

We have to crack down not only on the way sentences get handed down in court-rooms but also on what happens after that. Why, for example, do we let criminals out early for good behavior? Shouldn't crimi-nals be expected to behave in prison? I think they should set it up so that if your sentence is three years and you misbehave, you'll do five! That's the mind-set we need.

And I don't think we need to work so hard at making criminals comfortable, either. Basic needs should be met, yes. Anything less would be inhumane. But I'm against these "country club" prisons where they get cable TV and computers and workout rooms — the kinds of things that a lot of hardworking, law-abiding citizens can't even afford. It shouldn't be more comfort-able to be in prison than it is to be out.

The death penalty

My dad always used to say, "How come life in prison don't mean life?" That's a good question. Because until it does, we're not ready to do away with the death penalty in this country. Stop thinking in terms of "punishment" for a minute and think in terms of safeguarding innocent people from incorrigible murderers. Americans have a right to go about their lives without worrying about these people being back out on the street. So until we can make sure they're off the streets permanently, we have to grit our teeth and put up with the death penalty. So we need to work toward making a life sentence meaningful again. If life meant life, I could, if you'll excuse the pun, live without the death penalty.

We don't have it here in Minnesota, thank God, and I won't advocate to get it. But I will advocate to make life in prison mean life. I don't think I would want the responsibility for enforcing the death penalties, and while I'm governor, people would always be coming to me to commute them. That's a heavy responsibility to have on your shoulders. I've thought about this. There's always the inevitable question of whether someone you gave the order to execute might truly have been innocent. It would weigh on you pretty drastically if you ever made a mistake. That's the kind of thing I would have to face on a pretty regular basis if we had the death penalty here.

Of course, for that one part of me that is glad to be relieved of that responsibility, there's another part of me that hears about these brutal mass murderers and thinks, "Gee, maybe I'd like to walk over and pull the switch." Would that be a "hands-on" governor?

Drunk driving

There's no question that we need tougher drunk-driving laws for repeat offenders. We need to take a lesson from European countries, where driving isn't a right but a privilege. There isn't a person on this planet by this time who doesn't know that when you consume alcohol you shouldn't get behind the wheel of a car. The people who do it anyway should have their privilege to drive taken away.

Marijuana

Our government has the weirdest bias against cannabis. There's no reason for everybody to be so afraid of it. It's not the antichrist the DEA makes it out to be. Industrial hemp is a very useful plant. Canada has figured this out; they're growing hemp already. So what's the matter with us? I challenged the attorney general to get rid of the criminal stigma associated with hemp so we can look at it in terms of how it might be useful: as an alternative fuel, as a paper source, as a fiber for clothing, or as anything else that might be productive. I believe that God put everything on the earth for a reason. I don't think cannabis is here just so we can eradicate it.

I also think the government has no business telling us what we can and can't use for pain relief and in matters of our own health. There are indicators from medical studies that show marijuana can help ease the suffering of people with cancer and AIDS. There's just no good reason for denying it. The ban on medical marijuana exists for no other reason than the government's bias. There are plenty of more addicting painkillers out there, legal and readily available.

And if making the stuff illegal was truly going to stop people from using it, wouldn't it have done so by now? Americans should already have learned that lesson. There are some things it's better not to try to legislate, because it doesn't work. I remember my mom comparing the prohibition of drugs to the prohibition of alcohol. She lived through

Prohibition, and she told me that the same thing is happening with drugs today: All you do by making it illegal is make the gangsters rich. As long as there's a demand for it, we're not going to be able to eliminate the supply. My answer to the problem is, let's regulate it! Let's collect some tax money off of it!

Prostitution and drug possession

With as grave a situation as we're facing with inner-city crime and the rising crime rate among juveniles, we shouldn't be wasting so much time and so many resources on prosecuting consensual crimes such as prostitution and drug possession. It should be pretty obvious by now that these are the kinds of social problems that legislation can't touch. I'm saying we should regulate drugs and prostitution. Those would be more effective ways to handle them.

If you really feel strongly about stopping these kinds of activities, the most effective thing you can do is to work with at-risk individuals yourself, to stop them before they begin. And that kind of prevention doesn't take government programs. It takes you. Volunteering.

Drug dealing

I hold drug possession and drug dealing

as two totally different concepts. The drug dealers who resort to deadly street violence should be dealt with severely as the criminals they are.

But we have to become willing to admit as a nation that our war against drugs has failed. And we have to start looking for other solutions. I want the drug business stopped. But I know it never will stop as long as people want the drugs. It's supply and demand. The suppliers are so ruthless they can get into any market. You can even get drugs in prison.

But if there was no more demand for drugs, gangs and drug dealers would be out of business. I think the key lies in keeping young people from becoming their customers in the first place. If parents get involved, and if schools educate young people about the dangers of drugs, we can dry up the drug dealers' customer base. That's how we win the war.

Gun control

I'm all for gun control, I just define it a little differently. If you can put two rounds into the same hole from twenty-five meters, that's gun control! But if you're going to own a gun, you have an obligation to know what you're doing with it. When the Constitution gave us the right to bear arms, it also made us responsible for using them properly. With the right comes the responsibility. It's not fair of us as citizens to lean more heavily on one side of that equation than on the other.

So I support waiting periods and training requirements for gun ownership, and I like the idea that it shouldn't be incredibly easy to get guns. I support the right to carry concealed weapons, but I think people who want a concealed-weapons permit need to pass a training and safety course, and they need to be able to display a high level of competence with their weapon, both at the time of licensing and periodically thereafter.

Where I draw the line is at gun registration. A law that says that everybody who owns a gun has to be on record is too easy to abuse. We have a bad history in this country of singling people out for the wrong reasons, and there's no guarantee we won't do it again in the future. Case in point: Do you know who was the last political leader to insist that every gun owner be registered with the government? Hitler.

Gun control is no small issue. It was so important to our Founding Fathers that they built the right to bear arms into the Constitution. But what people often forget today is that the Constitution also calls for people who choose to bear arms to be part of a "well-regulated militia." In other words, you need to know how to use your weapon, to practice with it, and to belong to a group of shooters who support each other's integrity. How many gun owners submit themselves to that kind of regulation today?

Our forefathers deemed that if you want the right you must take up the responsibility. Of course, we need to keep guns out of the hands of people who have forfeited that right — namely, criminals. The gun problem we have in this country is not the fault of the guns, it's the fault of the people who are misusing them. Let's put the blame for this problem where it belongs: on the person who pulls the trigger.

Abortion

I don't support abortion. I could never participate in one. But I think it would be a mistake to make them illegal again. Prohibition doesn't mean something's going away. People who think it's going to stop just because we legally prohibit it are fooling themselves. What criminalization will do is force women into garages and back alleys, and then you're going to have two lives in jeopardy. My mom, who was a nurse, used to talk about the messes that would come in after back-alley abortions went wrong, which they often did. The way to stop abortion is to deal, philosophically and spiritually, with the people who get them. And that's not something that government can touch.

This issue is far more complicated than it seems. In those rare cases in which the mother's life is at risk if the pregnancy continues, making this a legislative decision takes it out of the hands of doctors and clergy, who are the ones that are qualified to make it. You're also taking it out of the hands of families, who then face the loss of a loved one.

Welfare: The government is not a charity

The government is not a charity institution. Constitutionally, there's nothing supporting the idea that people have a right to expect charity from the government. I believe in charity, I believe in helping out our fellow people when they're down. But I also believe that government programs funded by tax money are about the worst possible way to help out people in need. Private charities are much better, and here's why: People can get involved in the ones that are most meaningful to them. They can volunteer and make a difference, not just with the money they donate but with a part of themselves. They can get involved personally. If you needed help, wouldn't you rather deal with them than with a sterile, bureaucratic government institution? Private charity given freely from the heart is more effective than "forced" charity from the government.

Statistically, when the economy is good, charity donations are good too. All on their own, people will give to charity. When they can, people will help out other people, without having the government acting as a middleman. So government's role should be to work on keeping the economy strong.

Doesn't it then make sense that we do all that we can to keep government spending to a minimum? So that the average citizen has more financial power to invest in charities? In giving the tax surplus back, we empower taxpayers even further to decide what charities they want to donate to.

Now, I do understand that there's a difference between the hard-core, bare-bones, Constitutional definition of what government is supposed to do and the way it is in reality. In recent times, we've made government take on this function of charity, and at this point that role is so ingrained into its fiber that we might not be able to remove it even if we tried. And if that's truly how Americans want their government to be, so be it.

But I get very disturbed when I see people demonstrating with signs that say "Welfare Rights." There is nothing in the Constitution that says you have a right to welfare!

Do you know what welfare is? It's taking money from someone who is working to give to someone who's not! I think the people that require the government to do that for them are selfish. I don't know about you, but my conscience wouldn't allow me to do that. I couldn't live with myself if I knew I was taking money from someone who was working hard when I myself wasn't willing to work.

The right-sized social safety net

Now, I do believe there's a place in government for a safety net of some kind. Of course, if someone is truly unable to work at all, we take care of them. The government has the same obligation to people who can't pay taxes as it does to those who can. That's a social obligation. When you were too young to pay taxes, you got some of the benefits of government, just as you did if you were ever too sick to work, just as you will when you become too elderly to work. I get angry at the people who say, "I have no children! Why do I have to pay for education?" Well, besides the fact that you reap enormous benefits (most of which you probably never even realize) from living in a society where the people around you are educated, you yourself got an education, and somebody paid for you!

Public education is for the common good. You might end up helping to pay for someone to go to school who later becomes a research scientist and finds a cure for a disease you have. In reality it's not often that direct, but that's the gist of the idea. For the common good, we want people to be educated.

You have to be pretty bad off not to be able to do anything productive. Most people can do something. We've only recently begun to realize how productive the disabled can be, if given the chance. People who have work to do are healthier.

Maybe we should set welfare up so that it makes up the gap between what someone needs to live on and what they're able to earn. There are any number of needs in society that someone who is trying to ease back into the workforce can fill. For example, I think we need to have monitors on public-school buses. The driver's job is to drive. Somebody else needs to be on board to keep the kids under control. It's a great opportunity for someone to gain people skills and experience. They'd be contributing something to the community in exchange for the money they're receiving, and they're receiving skills they can build on. I believe everyone should have a job to do, no matter how modest, whether it's delivering papers or shining shoes. There is honor in all honest work.

But here again is a place where government is simply not going to be effective: Who determines who is in need? Who determines how much they should or can earn? Who decides how much a given person needs to get by on? Who determines whether they can or can't work? Ultimately, in most situations, the individual decides whether or not they "can" work, and the government just has to accept it. We have to find a realistic way to determine and define these things, or we will end up with a growing monster like the one we have now. There should be some kind of minimal safety net. But our government has turned a safety net into a lifestyle choice.

The Constitution guarantees you only a very few rights. You have the right to live free, go out, and compete. You have the right to life, liberty, and the pursuit of happiness. It doesn't say you have the right to be given money you didn't earn. And it certainly doesn't say you have a right to reproduce when you can't provide for that child and do your social duty by that child for a minimum of eighteen years. We don't have the right to bear children and then make them wards of the state. When Terry and I first got married, I was wrestling. We had no money, and we lived on the road. We couldn't have raised a child. So we waited five years, until we had settled down and bought a house.

I think that as a society we have an obligation to help out when someone truly needs help. I'm a big believer in charity. I give to a number of charities; I show up at a bunch of charitable functions each year, and I know that most people do that. Most people will give generously, of their own free will, when they have the chance. But don't abuse it by saying you have a right to their generosity!

I have a lot of hope for this new generation coming up, the young folks who played such a big role in getting me elected. It's probably too late for it to happen in my lifetime, but that's one of the things I'm urging them to work for in their lifetime: get the government out of the role of charity and back to a manageable size.

Prevailing wage versus living wage

Both prevailing wages and living wages are well-intentioned, but they're two entirely different concepts. A prevailing wage deals with government policy when the government is doing the hiring. When it's acting in accord with the prevailing wage, the government bids out contracts to people and supports unions and what unions stand for. It makes sense for the government to set a fair wage for government work. It's good business.

A living wage, on the other hand, does nothing but make government grow and the economy suffer. With a mandated living wage, the government dictates to businesses what they have to pay their employees. Hypothetically speaking, if you get a job at five dollars an hour, and the government comes along and tells your employer to pay you seven, guess who's going to get at least seventy cents of that extra two bucks? The government! And what happens when government gets more money? It grows! If the government really and truly feels that strongly about you having more money for the work you do, why doesn't it just let you keep more of the money you pay in taxes? We have to avoid policies that blindly make government grow.

Moreover, there's evidence to show that a rise in the living wage costs jobs. I think this issue should be left up to the employee. If you don't think a job pays enough, don't take it! It's called individual choice. No one makes you take that job; no one puts a hammerlock on you and makes you accept a wage you don't think is suitable.

Health care

Government's interference in health care should be kept to a minimum. The government shouldn't be telling physicians how to practice. What works for one doctor might not work for another. The government tends to be too cautious in the regulation of some drugs. We should find ways to expedite the process of getting experimental drugs onto the market. If a drug might save a dying person's life, it should be up to the physician and his patient, not the government, to determine whether the risk is justified.

I do see a good argument in favor of government-funded immunizations. It's called prevention. The cost of immunizing schoolchildren against common communicable diseases such as flu, chicken pox, and whooping cough is insignificant compared to the cost of treating them when they get sick. Plus, it would save some misery and a lot of lost school days. This is an example of something government should do for the good of society.

Socialized medicine might work as an interim measure, to get us all back on track, but in the long run I think it would be disastrous for our economy. Nothing pushes prices down and quality up like competition. I think privatization is the best way to make the medical profession behave as it should.

What I Bring to the Table

I can't possibly tackle all this in four years. I only have a limited amount of time to make a difference, and if I spread myself too thin, I won't be effective at any of it. So I've picked a handful of issues that I'm going to focus on while I'm here. They're the three that I think will have the greatest effect on all the other problems and challenges we face.

I'm going to do what I can to reform the tax system, because the government takes too much of our money and spends too much of it inappropriately. I'm going to focus on reforming our public-school system and help get families reinvested in their neighborhood schools, because with better education and more parental and community support, kids will be far less vulnerable to most of the social problems we face today. And I'm going to keep on encouraging people to get involved in their government, to do their part to make it what they think it should be. Because that's the truly great thing about our system of government: It's ours.

During the four years that I serve as governor, I promise that the one thing you'll always get from me is honesty. You might not always like what I have to say. But I'll speak my mind. And if I don't know the answer to something, I'll do my best to find it out.

I have nothing to hide; I am who I am. I got elected governor just by being who I am, so I owe it to the people who voted for me to keep on being me. I come from working-class origins, and my values reflect that. I believe in simplicity, hard work, and independence. I love a challenge. I love living life to the fullest. I've worked hard for everything I've achieved. I've taken risks along the way, and I have very few regrets. The story of how I got here is bigger than me; it's bigger than any one person. If you want to understand where I'm coming from, read on.

CHAPTER 3

HOW IT ALL STARTED

Hot lights. The smell of sweat. And the crowd, packed to capacity. The fighters step into the ring, glaring at each other with barely concealed rage. Teeth clench. Nostrils flare. It's a grudge match, and I have to hold up my hands to keep them separated until the bell.

"I want a clean fight," I tell them. "Understand?"

The fighters nod, grunt, not breaking eye contact with each other. I step back. This crowd is going wild. They're bloodthirsty, screaming for action. I can't blame them. I ring the bell.

The fight begins. Punches fly back and forth. There's some ducking, some dodging, some fancy footwork. A punch connects lightly, rocking one fighter's head to the side, but he keeps going.

Suddenly, one fighter grabs his opponent, swings him through the air, and slams him down. And sits on him. The opponent scrambles free and grabs the first fighter by the hair. They tumble across the ring until the first fighter ends up on top, swings his fist free, and pops his opponent squarely in the snout.

The opponent bursts into tears. "Knock it off!" he sobs. "Jimmy, make him quit!" And suddenly, the match is over.

Welcome to the Saturday-afternoon fights — sixth-grade style. I'd put together a makeshift "ring" in my parents' basement, then I'd match up different combinations of my classmates. I set the fights up, refereed them, and went head-to-head in more than a few of them myself. Of course, the thought didn't cross my mind then that I might someday choose something like this as a profession. This was just the kind of thing you did for fun if you were a kid growing up on the South Side of Minneapolis, Minnesota.

Why Minnesota? To this day I can't tell you why my grandparents chose to move there. I do know what made my dad's parents decide to leave Pennsylvania, where they'd settled after they moved to this country from Czechoslovakia. They were getting away from the coal mines. My grandfather had worked in the mines, and it didn't take him long to figure out that they were killers. They left because they wanted to improve their lot in life — better work and better lives for their children.

The first lesson I ever got about my origins came from my Aunt Betty. She was ancient even at that time, and she's ninety-three today. Somebody was asking me what nationality I was, and I said, "I'm Czech." Aunt Betty whirled in her chair and growled, "You are not! You're Slovak!" Apparently, Czechs lived in the city, and Slovaks lived in the country. My family was from the country. She wanted me to know my origins and be proud of them.

I never got to know my dad's parents. They died while he was off serving in World War II. I knew my mom's folks, though; they were William and Martha Lenz. They were of German origin. William was a builder. My mom has shown me houses around Iowa that he built. Martha was a typical grandmother with a big garden.

My mom and dad, Bernice and George, were introduced by somebody my mom referred to only as "the Colonel." They were both army people. My dad was in a tank-destroyer division; my mom was an army nurse, and this colonel was somebody she worked with.

Still, the odds were against them tying the knot. My father never had any intention of getting married until he was forty. There's some kind of bachelor strain running through my dad's side of the family — an independent streak, a taste for not having to answer to anybody. My Aunt Betty never married. My brother Jan's never been to the altar either, and I'm sure he never will be. He just doesn't want it. It doesn't fit with his lifestyle. Aunt Betty used to chew him out for it: "Don't you want to get married and have a nice family like your brother?" And he'd say, "Well what about you? How come you didn't?" Jan's fifty now — single for life.

My dad made it to age forty before he married, and my mom was thirty. They were both very focused on their careers. He was an enlisted man, but she was an officer, a lieutenant. In fact, that's what he called her whenever they got into a spat. He'd say, "Ah, the lieutenant's on my case again. . . . What the hell is them officers' problem anyway?" They both took their time coming to the point where they were ready for marriage. But, lucky for me, they eventually got there.

I was born on July 15, 1951, three years after my brother Jan. And in case you were thinking *Ventura* doesn't sound like a very Czechoslovakian name, I'll tell you that nowhere on my birth certificate will you find the name *Ventura,* or *Jesse,* or *The Body.* I was born James George Janos, and that's the name I went by until I decided to become a professional wrestler nearly twenty-five years later.

My brother and I inherited our dad's genetic tendency toward independence, but our mom also taught us to stand on our own two feet, to think and do for ourselves, and not to be reliant on other people. Dad was easygoing to a fault. He was strong and a powerful swimmer, another trait that he passed on to me. He could swim across the Mississippi and back. None of his friends could do that. But for all his strength, he never struck us or handled us roughly. My mom took care of that aspect, though — she'd get after us with a razor strap. She was the disciplinarian. But even though my dad never laid a hand on us, there was a quiet strength in him, an authority we didn't have the guts to test. If we got out of line, just hearing his footsteps on the stairs was enough to make us behave. I learned from him that sometimes strength doesn't need to flaunt itself — it simply is, and people recognize that.

He really enjoyed life to the fullest, and I think there's a lot of him in me. I think too that I've passed some of both of my folks on

72

to my son, Tyrel, consciously or not, because he's really into the experience of life, and at nineteen he's already out following his own road and doing his own thing. My wife, Terry, agrees that there's a lot of me in him.

And my father was something else besides. He was a hero. At my dad's funeral, a friend of the family told a story about a car wreck that my dad had happened upon. The car was burning, and people were trapped inside. My dad went in and pulled the people to safety. No hesitation. He saved the lives of everyone in the car, and then he just walked off. He didn't even stick around to accept the accolades. That was the kind of guy he was. Hearing that story gave me a very vivid sense of the kind of man my father was. He wouldn't think of himself as a hero — and in a sense, that's what made him great. In a crisis situation, he could impulsively do what had to be done.

Sometimes, though, my father's impulsiveness took unexpected turns. My mom, the more disciplined of the two, used to have a stash of money she'd save up for new cars. She liked to buy a new car every four years, and she always paid cash. She didn't believe in buying anything on credit. There was never a car payment in our house.

But one time when I was about seven, my

dad sneaked into that stash and used the money to buy a piece of lakefront property. Of course, he had to come home after the deed was done and fess up. We all tensed for the explosion.

"Well," Mom said finally, "we'll just have to make do with the old car for a while."

We couldn't believe it. Instead of tearing our family apart, my father's impulsiveness somehow pulled us together. My grandfather helped us build a cabin on that land. It was a great time. The whole family went out there, all the cousins and everybody, and pitched tents while we built it. Everybody helped out. Even we little kids got to pound some nails. One night a storm blew in off the lake, and we were afraid the wind would rip the tents right off of us. It was great fun. We still have that cabin today — a dubious business decision transformed into a family legacy.

Now, I've got strong political opinions, and they took root early. Both of my folks could be very stubborn and bullheaded, but my dad was politically so. My first introduction to politics came early in life, over family dinners. We watched the news on the TV while we ate, and he argued back to it whenever he heard something he didn't like. He ranted and raved and carried on to the point where my mom was ready to toss him down to the basement.

He'd get fired up, and he loved to talk about it. He hated all politicians. He didn't have too many kind things to say about any of them or about the government. My father referred to Hubert Humphrey as "Old Rubber-Lip." His name for Richard Nixon was "The Tailless Rat." I was watching TV with him the day of Nixon's famous "I am not a crook" speech.

My dad looked at Nixon on the TV and said, "Look, you can see the son of a bitch is lying."

I looked at him. "Come on, Dad. How do you know that?"

"Because anyone with sweat on their upper lip is lyin' to you."

Sure enough, whenever he was doing an important speech, Nixon always got this line of sweat on his upper lip.

I truly believe that my father developed his deep hatred for Nixon because he voted for him. My dad was a staunch Democrat; the old-fashioned, farmer/laborer, working-man's Democrat. He never would admit it, but I think he voted for Nixon just to vote against Kennedy, because, like many people at the time, he was afraid that if they put a Catholic in office, the pope would be running the country.

My father vehemently opposed Vietnam. He'd say, "Ah, that Viet-nan. That thing's no good. Somebody's makin' money." He was a street-smart, blue-collar guy with an eighth-grade education, and he called it "Viet-nan." But he'd say, "That's the only reason we're there, because somebody's makin' money." And by God, I think he was right.

Like me, my father was a patriotic man; like me, he was a veteran. But what he taught me was that the country was us, the people, not the government. I would come home from school with my head full of what they'd taught me in class, and I'd argue with him about the domino effect of communism. And my father said, "Bullshit. There ain't no domino effect." And he was right. We ended up losing that war, but it was communism that ultimately collapsed.

My parents were the biggest influences on me in my early years, of course, but I also had a sixth-grade teacher that I really liked named Helen Dunphy. Just before my class left sixth grade, she made predictions about what each one of us would turn out to be. She predicted that I would be a sportscaster after I retired from the ring. She was referring to boxing rather than wrestling, but otherwise she was dead-on.

In those days, you got very close to your grade-school teachers. South Minneapolis in general was a close-knit community back then. It was a great time to live there. You could roam around and do anything you wanted with great freedom, with none of the fear that city kids grow up with today. Nobody worried about where their children were. We'd just tell our folks we were going down to the river for the day, and off we'd go and not come back until dinner. And they had no fear. My dad actually got me interested in the river, because he himself had grown up playing around on the banks of the Mississippi.

I met up with Helen Dunphy about thirty years later, after I had made it big in wrestling. One of my classmates had kept the sheet of paper that she'd written down all her predictions on. And I decided to go over and look her up and have a reunion with her. She was in her last year of teaching before she retired. She didn't believe it when I showed up unannounced for a visit. She had her foot in a cast at the time, so she had sent a kid over to answer the classroom intercom. I told the kid, "Tell Mrs. Dunphy that Jim Janos, Jesse 'The Body' Ventura, is here."

I heard her voice in the background saying, "Come on!"

The principal leaned in and said, "No, you better tell her he's here. I'm looking at him!"

She was a very popular teacher who really loved her kids and took the extra step — the kind of teacher who makes all the difference. She probably never knew how much of an influence she was in my life. She was thrilled to see me that day. We sat together and reminisced all afternoon. It was one of those rare moments when you can tell the person looking at you isn't just seeing you the way you are now — she was seeing me the way I'd been back then, too.

But you can't get a good sense of what's at the core of who I am until I tell you about the South Side Boys. These were the guys I grew up with in South Minneapolis. I met most of these guys in grade school, and we ended up forming friendships that have lasted a lifetime. My dad had the same kind of lifelong friendships with the group of guys he grew up with; they were friends to the grave. My son doesn't have that, and I feel bad for him. I'm still in touch with these guys today; they're still very much a part of my life. They keep me in touch with reality. They connect me to my past. They keep my feet on the ground.

The South Siders came and went; there

were anywhere from five of us to twenty-five. But there was always a core group that I was a part of, and different people from time to time orbited around that core. Kevin Johnson and I met in kindergarten. Kevin's father, Eddie, was the one who told the story about my dad saving the lives of those people in the burning car. There was Ricky Bjornson; he's still a South Sider at heart, even though we kind of drifted apart in high school. We started hanging with different crowds because I was more of an athlete and he wasn't. But he came to the party after my inauguration. He was my best friend in elementary school. There was Lynn Wagner and Jim Hovey. Steve Nelson became a major part of the core group of South Siders, and he played a pivotal role in where I went with my life. But he didn't come into the picture until later.

In fifth grade, Jerry Flatgard moved into the neighborhood. He became my best friend. To this day, it doesn't matter how long we've been away from each other; whenever we get back together, it's like no time has passed. That's the true test of friendship. I was in Jerry's bed when I lost my virginity on New Year's Eve when I was sixteen. That's a pretty good indicator of a close friendship. But don't worry, Jerry wasn't with me. We weren't that close!

We were like the Three Musketeers, me and Ricky and Jerry. We'd all made bets on who would be the first to "do it." They both assumed that I wouldn't be the one, because I wasn't as aggressive with females as they were. But I had been dating a girl who I'd picked up on Lake Street (our *Happy Days/ American Graffiti* street, where guys with hot cars cruised around and picked up girls and took them to drive-ins). She and I had gotten so far along that we were about ready to do it in a car. But I wanted my first time to be special; I didn't want it to be in a car. Jerry's folks were out of town that night, and we were having a party, so I brought her inside and took her into Jerry's bed. And when I brought her downstairs to take her home, I waited until her back was turned to give Jerry and Ricky the nod, to let them know I'd won the bet. And it was funny, but after that night, I was never again with her. It was just one of those things.

We had all gone to Cooper Grade School together and then to Sanford Junior High. But then in high school, we got divided. I lived on Thirty-second Street. For whatever reason, if you lived on the north side of Thirty-second Street, you had to go to South High School. If you lived on the south side, as I did, you went to Roosevelt. So one half went to South, and my half went to Roosevelt. But it was remarkable; we always maintained our friendship. We went to rival high schools and played against each other, but on the weekends we hung out together. We were the South Side Guys. We were the 1960s' version of the Little Rascals.

We always used to sleep out in the back-yard in tents. But as soon as our folks were in bed, we were up and out of the tents, running the streets all night. We stayed out until two or three in the morning, and we were only in sixth grade. We stuck stuff in our sleeping bags so it looked like we were sleeping. We took off in hopes that our parents wouldn't come out and catch us gone. And miraculously, they never did. Thank God. If my kids behaved the way I did, there'd be a lot more gray hair on my head.

We were adventurers. We roamed the river-bank. And we drank. In that era, that's what you did. This was early junior high school. We'd go down to the sandbar on the Missis-sippi riverbank on Saturday and Sunday mornings, because the older kids always had beer parties on Friday and Saturday nights. If you went down there early the next morning, you could always find a few beers lying in the sand, ones they'd lost during the night. We had a little cave where we hid them. Then when we accumulated about thirty of them, on a Saturday we'd tell our families we were going to the river all day.

We'd go down at eight or nine in the morning, dig up our stash of scavenged beer, and start drinking. We'd get drunk. Ricky had some kind of stomach problem, so when he got drunk he'd go into projectile puking. He'd spew like a firehose into the river, and we'd laugh. And then by noon it was time to start sobering up so we could go home. By the time we went home around six or seven at night, we'd be sober. We went through the whole period of getting drunk and getting sober without passing out or going to sleep. It was strange. As an adult, at some point you usually sleep it off. But we didn't want to miss any of it.

We started out that way, being pretty wild kids. We've never really grown up. We still misbehave when we get together. It's just in us. Jerry and I ended up getting labeled. It was always "The Jerry and Jim Show." We would find someone to pick on, and we'd have fun with them. The other South Siders speculated about who would fall prey to us.

There was a teacher in junior high named Mr. Steele, whom we hated. We thought of him as a little wimpy guy who tried to act tough. We never respected him. One night we built a stuffed replica of him. We put a sign on it to make sure there was no mistake about who it was supposed to be. Then we traveled the alleyways until we found an aluminum stepladder, and we stole it. We took it over to the school and hung Mr. Steele in effigy from the flagpole. When we were done, we couldn't decide what to do with the ladder, so we pitched it through the school window.

We weren't juvenile delinquents; I wouldn't put it that way. We just had a streak of mischief in us. And if one of us dared the other to do something, it would happen. It was just one of those things. I remember back when we used to go up to the lake and pitch tents in the woods, we would always stash some kind of liquor in our sleeping bags. One time, Jerry was bragging that the only way to drink was to drink like a man, which meant you didn't use any mix. So to prove it, he drank a whole pint of Fleischmann's straight. Boy, did he pay for it the next day. We were lying out on the shore the next day, and every ten minutes he'd have to roll over and dry heave. And the whole time he had to try to hide it from my mom.

We were all tough. We never backed down

from anybody. We weren't above defending our turf when we had to. But we weren't a gang, as you think of gangs today. There were gangs in Minneapolis at that time, but we weren't part of that at all. Nobody carried guns and knives in those days. Kids on the street didn't kill each other the way they do, sadly, today. If you had a problem to settle, you settled it with skin.

Of course, we did what we could to make sure that when it came down to skin, we could make an impression. In shop class we made what were called "fist-loads," on the sly. The shop had big lengths of tube steel, welding rods. Whenever the teacher wasn't around, we cut off a big piece of it, and Jerry hid it in his pants. We took it home and cut it into four-inch lengths that fit inside our fists. When you hit somebody when you're holding a fist-load, it's much more effective. It makes your fist much heavier. You can take somebody down real easy with a fist-load. When my dad was a kid, you just put a roll of quarters in your hand and it did the same thing.

We always carried our fist-loads in our pockets in case the need ever arose. And it did from time to time. We all had our own turf, and if anybody invaded your turf, you had to defend it. Remember, this was in

1962 or '63, before the Beatles came to America and launched a cultural revolution. This was before the hippies, before the era of love and peace. One time, this kid named Billy Fritz was throwing snowballs at Jerry's sister after school. Like any junior high-school kid, Jerry had no great liking for his sister. If he'd been the one picking on her, probably nobody would have thought twice. But woe unto anyone else who messed with her. After all, she was his sister. So Jerry calmly took a dog chain, wrapped it around his fist, came up to Billy Fritz, and pow! Billy's face just exploded. But in those days, you didn't get busted or labeled for that kind of thing. If you got beat up, you didn't run home and cry to your parents, and you didn't call the police. It was just part of life. You accepted it.

In those days, it was good to have an older brother. I had Jan, and Jerry had Dennis (who is today a sergeant in the Minneapolis police department). An older brother meant you had access to more stuff. When Dennis went to college, we bargained our way into the wild frat parties he and his friends had every weekend by promising to clean up the next day. We passed ourselves off as college students to the coeds. We were sixteen.

When you have an older brother, you tend

to follow him in everything he does. He became an athlete; I became an athlete. He got into swimming; I got into swimming. He became a swimming captain; I became a swimming captain. And then later he became a SEAL. It wasn't until after the service that Jan and I started to go off on different paths.

An older brother can teach you a lot about passing yourself off as older than you are. One day in high school, we got out of class for teacher conferences, and we decided to have a party in the daytime. We were sixteen, and the drinking age was twenty-one. We all threw all our money together and drove down to Mary's liquor store near Twenty-seventh. I put on an army jacket and a pair of shades, and I walked in in broad daylight and ordered three cases of beer and assorted liquor.

When I walked in, the guy behind the counter said, "You in the army?"

I said, "Nah. I just got discharged. I was stationed in Germany."

He asked, "We still got a lot of troops in Germany?"

I said, "Oh, yeah, quite a few." Totally bullshitting him. I bought so much stuff I had to wheel it out to the car on a dolly. They never carded me, in spite of the fact that I paid for all that beer with a fistful of crumpled-up one-dollar bills and change. We weren't smart enough to go to a bank first and change it into bigger bills!

A lot of the South Side Guys ended up going into the military, oddly enough. We wrote to each other when we were in the service. We all got back about the same time. When we got home, we reunited. And even though we'd all grown up in different ways and were changed a lot by our different experiences in the service, our friendships were as strong as ever.

At that point we were all starting to go off in different directions to live our own lives, but we knew we would find some way to come together and get back in touch with our roots on a regular basis. And that's when the annual Knife River trip started. As we've progressed together through life, we get together every spring when the smelt are running and head off into the wilderness for our own South Side version of a male bonding ritual. No women have ever been allowed. No women will ever be allowed. I haven't been able to make it to all of them, but I have flown in from as far as Tampa, Florida, to get there.

At first we went to the Knife River near Duluth, but after a while that started to get too crowded, and we couldn't misbehave enough. So we started going to a place called Lake Sullivan, and when that got overrun we went all the way up to McDougal Lake, north of Two Harbors, right near the Canadian border, in the middle of nowhere.

We go for three or four days, out into the wilderness. The original excuse was that we were going fishing. But one year about fourteen of us went up there with one set of waders, no net, and one license. That's how serious we were about catching fish. It's about letting loose. It's roughing it. It's Minnesotan.

It's the kind of trip where every waking moment you have a beer in your hand. Over the years, we've progressed from sleeping on the ground to sleeping in tents. Now that we're all fairly successful, we rent mobile homes, which as we get older is a lot better, because if the weather is bad, we can just sit comfortably in the mobile homes. We drive up there with generators and stereos and tons of fireworks. We string lights through the trees, and we shoot off all our fireworks and play our rock 'n' roll until all hours of the night. And up there you can play it as loud as you want because it's way out in the middle of the woods. There's probably not another living soul around for ten miles. The only things we disturb are the deer and the bears.

We even had a sheriff walk into the camp one time. There we were, bodies strewn everywhere, in different stages of stupor. He looked around at the lights and all our stuff, and he said, "You guys call this camping?" And we said, "Hell, yeah! This is South Side camping!" And he just shook his head and left. He knew we weren't harming anything.

So those are the South Siders. They're lifelong friends. I know that no matter what I do in life, they're there to bring me back to reality. They're my reality check. They know me as Jim Janos, the kid down the block who grew up with them. And I'll always be him. Of all the people in my life, they're the proudest of what I've accomplished. But they keep me grounded. If you'd have told us back then that I'd end up the governor . . .

I always remember that power can corrupt, so that's one of the reasons I'm thankful for the South Side Boys. They would never let me get too far out of line. They've done so much to keep me focused on who I am. I have them to thank for giving me such a solid base to push off into life from. It makes it a lot easier to put yourself out there when you know you've got lifelong friends at home that you can always come back to. I have them to thank for a lot of where I've gotten in life.

But in particular, I have Steve Nelson to thank for getting me into the navy. He became part of the South Siders at a much later age. He was from a different neighborhood, but he went to Roosevelt and became a South Sider. To this day he's part of the core group. Steve's parents, Harold and Helen, raised him to be perfect: please and thank you. He had impeccable manners. You never wanted to bring him to your house, because his behavior was so good that as soon as he left your parents would say to you, "How come you don't act like Steve?" Because of that, he took the brunt of the Jerry and Jim Show. Steve was such a great guy, we decided that we just couldn't let him go through life that perfect. It was our mission. We had to corrupt him.

So when I was about sixteen, I went into Shinder's, the famous bookstore, and I bought two or three soft-core porn magazines. Those days, there was no other kind of pornography around. You couldn't get what's out there today. I got away with it because I always looked older than I was. Jerry and I put them in a plain brown envelope, and we typed up Steve's name and address and a bunch of phony numbers up the side so it would look like a subscription. And we mailed it to him.

So Steve was sitting down to dinner with Harold and Helen the night this thing showed up in the mail. And of course they were curious to see what was inside this big package their son had gotten. So he ripped the top off and looked inside. They were sitting there watching him, so what could he do? He blurted out, "Oh, Jesus God, Mom and Dad . . . it's pornography!"

Of course, Helen was outraged. She was ready to go to war with the postmaster general. She wanted to launch a full investigation into whoever was allowing pornographic materials to come in the mail to her sixteen-year-old son. But Harold took the stuff into his bedroom to look it over, and Steve followed. Harold was a great old guy. He just scratched his head and looked at Steve and said, "God damn it, how come I don't get shit like this in the mail?"

Jerry and I knew this thing was going to arrive, so we had been going over there as much as we could, hoping to see what happened when it came. We got there that night, and Steve took us aside and whispered, "God, you're not going to believe what the hell happened!" We played dumb,

"What? What?" For twenty years we never told Steve we were the ones who did it. We were on one of our trips to the Knife River when Jerry and I finally decided we ought to fess up. Steve just swore at us, "You sons of bitches!" and laughed.

As kids, whenever we got Steve drunk, we'd bring him back home late at night. As soon as we got close to his house, we'd start laying on the horn, so we were sure to wake up his folks. We'd sling him over our shoulders and carry him to the door. And we'd ring the doorbell until Helen came down: "Harold! Harold! Steve's been drinking again!"

In those days, that's what you did. You drank. And it would generally lead you into trouble. Nothing serious, but you'd end up doing things you shouldn't do. Back in those days, drunk driving wasn't taken nearly as seriously as it is today. If the police caught you, they'd usually just take you home. I'm sure a lot of people died before it began to be taken as seriously as it should have been. But everyone was a lot more casual about that kind of thing in those days. You sowed your wild oats, and it was generally considered harmless. We packed a lot of fun into those years.

CHAPTER 4

NAVY SEALS

"All right. Which of you pukes has got flappers?"

"Mother" Moy came out with a table and set down a first-aid kit. It was the second day of training. I had taken forty-five minutes to run an obstacle course that was supposed to have been run in ten, and I had four or five raw, flapping blisters on each hand.

Like an idiot, I raised my hand. "I do, Moy!"

"Come on up here, boy!"

I figured he was going to put Mercurochrome on them, so I stepped up.

"Hold your hands out."

I put them out.

"Are you right-handed or left-handed?"

"Right-handed."

He nodded. "Lemme see your right hand."

I held it up. He grabbed every flap of skin and ripped them off, leaving my hand raw and throbbing. I had tears running down my face from the pain.

Do you know why he asked me whether I was right-handed or left-handed? Because when he was done, he said, "Now, you do the other hand." So I had to stand in front of the class with Moy and pull my own flappers off. When I was done, he said, "You big dummy, now get back in line."

Only six months earlier I'd been fresh out of high school, working for the highway department and partying with the South Side Guys. I was drifting along, not sure about what I wanted to do next.

I'd spent a lot of that summer of '69 feeling angry and betrayed. I'd been trying to qualify for a swimming scholarship to the University of Northern Illinois. I was good enough at swimming, for sure, but I couldn't get past the academic requirements. I was a good student academically, but I'd been taking the really tough college-prep courses: advanced algebra, trig, physics, chemistry. I thought that's what you did when you wanted to go to college.

I really did want to fulfill my parents' dream that I go to college. I would have been the only one in the family besides my mom to do it. I had the brains, and I eventually learned how to apply myself. I wasn't brilliant, but I was smart enough. Unfortunately, I was in classes with a bunch of geniuses on the fast track to becoming anesthesiologists and chemical engineers, the best of the best. Even so, I was doing OK. I was working really hard and making Bs and Cs. All my test scores were high enough to qualify for most programs.

But Northern Illinois expected you to be in the upper third of your class if you were an out-of-state student. I was only in the upper half, so I couldn't get past their admissions board. I felt betrayed, because if I'd taken the easier, slide-by courses like gym help, I could have made it into the program. But because I'd challenged myself and taken the tough stuff, I couldn't get in.

That's when my brother, Jan, who had joined the Navy SEALs a few years earlier, came home on leave from Da Nang. He pulled me and Steve aside in the backyard and warned us, "Don't join the service. Stay home. Go to college. Have fun. Don't get involved in this war."

By this time, it was unpopular to be part of the war. This was after the Tet offensive of 1968, a North Vietnamese military offensive that made even Walter Cronkite say that this war was now unwinnable. People were getting tired of seeing neighborhood kids coming home in boxes, dead from a war halfway around the world that nobody knew why we were fighting. We were told it was to stop communism, but now more people were forming other opinions, especially those in the schools and universities.

To truly understand the sixties, you had to have lived through the fifties, when every boy had short hair. Then all of a sudden, the Beatles came. It was like night and day. They created a rebellion of kids against parents that rose to a level that's never been seen since and will probably never be equaled. All of a sudden, guys grew their hair long and started looking, at least to their parents' generation, "like girls." Amazingly, girls' fashion changed the other way. Girls stopped wearing bras and makeup and went in for that "natural" look. The Beatles truly changed the world as we know it.

Marijuana was five dollars a bag. Back then, drugs were not a business; they were antiestablishment and provided escape. Young people switched from alcohol to hallucinogenic drugs. I smoked my first joint back in high school, but I was in the service and away from it all by the time the harder-core stuff became widely available.

There was such freedom in those days. A generation had turned its back on money and material things. All of a sudden, spirituality meant more than anything — it was all about friendship and brotherhood and sharing. The hit song that fall of '69 was Led Zeppelin's "Whole Lotta Love." Everybody shared whatever they had. Everybody hitchhiked wherever they wanted to go. People would take you in and let you sleep on the floor. It was an incredible time.

The sixties were phenomenal. I'm so lucky to have grown up in that time. I wouldn't trade it for anything. We were the most rebellious generation of this century.

Steve was drifting, like me. He had enrolled in college, but he wasn't really hip on it. It was September 11, 1969. He called me up out of the blue and said, "Jim, remember when we talked to Jan? I decided I want to do what he's doing. I want to join the SEALs. I want to go in the navy."

I said, "Steve, are you sure?"

Then he lowered the boom on me. He said, "And I want you to come with."

My jaw hit the floor. "Didn't you hear what Jan said? He told us not to do that!" We talked and argued back and forth.

Finally, he made me agree to go down to the recruiting office, and "just talk to 'em."

I gave in, "OK, but that's all I'm doing. We're just going to talk." So we went down to the recruiting office that afternoon. We talked to them. And we left with navy ID cards.

They pump you up. They're like car salesmen — it's like walking onto a lot and seeing a '64 GTO with three deuces and they tell you you can afford it! You're eighteen years old — what kind of defense do you have against that? That's their job! Their job is to be your best friend — until you enlist.

They even had what they called "the Buddy Program," where they would guarantee that you could go to boot camp with a friend, just in case the reason you weren't enlisting was that you didn't want to be out there alone for the first time in your life. When they found out we were interested in joining the Navy SEALs, they zeroed in: "Don't you want to be part of the most elite? The best of the best?"

I'd already had a taste of what it was like to be the best when I was into competitive swimming in high school. I was the first swimmer in the city of Minneapolis to ever break one minute in the hundred-yard butterfly. When I was a member of my high-school football team, we were undefeated. I always strove to do my best. So it was a challenge. Irresistible.

I had another reason for wanting to try for the SEALs: I had a dreadful fear of heights that I wanted to conquer. I knew the SEALs would force me to conquer that fear, and they did. You can't afford to be afraid of heights when you're fast-roping out of the hellhole of a helicopter. I ended up with thirty-four parachute jumps — you can't be too afraid of heights and jump out of airplanes! To this day, when I have fears, I always go out to conquer them. The only way to get rid of fear is to look it in the face and conquer it. I believe what Franklin Roosevelt said, that the only thing we have to fear is fear itself. I don't like to be afraid.

My folks were pretty upset when I told them we'd enlisted. They really hoped I would have a college career. My mom was especially hurt by it; she'd always seen me as the Son Who Would Go To College. I had come so close — I had enrolled in state college, but after I enlisted I had to ask for my money back. What could they do? I was eighteen; I could make my own decisions. Plus, I think when you're that age, sometimes you do things to hurt your parents a little. It's just natural; it's part of the whole separation process. And remember, this was 1969; it was the Era of Rebellion. So I think it was an act of rebellion in a way, to do what they didn't want me to do.

The navy gives you up to 120 days before you have to leave. I worked for the highway department for another month, saving up all my money. Then I quit, partied as much as I could, and had as much fun as I could squeeze in, right up until the last day. I was determined to leave home stone-cold broke, because I knew I wouldn't need any money where I was going.

We left on January 5, 1970. Ironically, the night after my inauguration, I had a dinner party at the governor's mansion with a bunch of friends, and Steve was there. At one point he raised his glass and announced, "You guys probably won't remember, but it was twenty-nine years to the day when Jim and I went off to the navy." We drank a toast to the day.

It was colder than hell that morning in 1970 when Steve and I left. We had gotten together with our friends and their parents the night before for one last party. A lot of us ended up joining the service, but Steve and I were the first. My mom drove me to the Federal Building in downtown Minneapolis and dropped me off. It was the last she was to see of me for a long time.

We had to check in by 5 A.M. Even that early, war protesters were camped out in front of the building, marching up and down with signs reading, "Hell No, Don't Go!" They rushed up to us, begging and pleading, "Don't go! Go to Canada! Don't join the service!"

We were sent down to navy boot camp in San Diego, and soon afterward we found ourselves standing in this hut in the middle of the night with some little shit yelling and screaming at us, when we could have been at home partying and chasing women. Instead, we were in for four years of this. That's when I decided — jokingly — that I was going to kill Steve.

We were Company 014. They shaved our heads and taught us how to fold our underwear.

In boot camp, part of your training is exposure to every facet of the navy. Different groups give you presentations. They teach you what an engineer does, what a signalman does, and so forth. Of course, Steve and I already knew what we wanted to do. We were there to be frogmen.

One day, we attended a presentation by the Navy SEAL Special Forces. There were three companies of us, about three hundred guys, at the presentation that day. All of a sudden, these guys walked in with spit-shined Cochrane jump boots and starched, tailored, skintight Marine greens — each of them with a look that said, You know I could kill you as soon as look at you. They started talking to us about being in the Navy SEALs Special Forces. They told us that you volunteered to try out, and if you made it through the training, you became one of them — the best the military had to offer. But they warned us it wouldn't be easy and that we would be physically and mentally tested beyond imagination. They also told us that we could quit at any time if we weren't good enough. They had my interest.

Then they showed us a film called *The Men with Green Faces*. In Vietnam, the SEALs were known as the Greenfaces, because they wore camouflage green and black on their faces and hands. The North Vietnamese feared the Greenfaces because they took jungle warfare into the NVA's own backyard — fighting them on their own terms and using their own tactics against them. Anything the NVA ever did to the Greenfaces, they got back even worse. Now my interest was really piqued!

When the film was over and the lights came up, the guys showing the movie said, "OK. Anyone who wants to volunteer to take the screen test to become a SEAL, stay here. The rest of you, get the fuck out of here." I saw guys running for the door. Regular navy "black shoes" wanted no part of this shit. Out of three hundred guys, forty or forty-five stayed. Steve and I were still in our seats.

They took us over to the swimming pool and started us on a series of physical tests, one after the other. The first part of the test called for you to swim three hundred meters using only an underwater recovery stroke, like the breaststroke or sidestroke. Then you paired off after the swimming and did as many pushups as you could in two minutes, as many sit-ups as you could in two minutes, and as many four-count "burpees" (squat thrusts) as you could in two minutes, and then you had to run a mile. If you quit at any time, that was it. It was all over. But they didn't tell you how many of each you had to do or how fast you had to run to pass.

Of course, I was fine with the swimming, because I was an ex–competitive swimmer. But like an idiot, I wanted to impress the SEAL instructors, so I went at it hard. I swam like hell. It didn't take long for me to learn that I should have paced myself; I should have taken my time and saved my strength. Steve did OK; he wasn't as strong a swimmer as I was, but I was ahead of everyone by a pool length.

Great finish in the pool. I was pumped. But then we did our push-ups, sit-ups, and burpees, one after the other, and by that time

I was blowing up. "My God," I thought, "I still have to run a mile." I thought I'd die before I got to the end; I was never a good runner anyway. But to my own amazement I finished third out of the group.

We started with about forty guys. Only twelve remained after the swimming. When we got all the way to the end, only four of us had passed: myself, Steve, and two others. Score two for the South Side Boys.

Of course, this was only in the fifth week of boot camp, and we still had six or seven weeks to go. So after passing the SEAL test, we had to return to our regular company and finish out boot camp before we could start our real training. Our company commander was Engineman First Class Pat Bondi. But as soon as he found out that we had passed the screen test and were volunteering for SEAL training, he pulled us aside, away from the rest of the guys in our company, and said, "You two guys really want to become pole-carrying assassins?"

That was the navy's slang term for the SEALs — the "pole" part came from the fact that as part of our boat-crew training at the mudflats we had to carry telephone poles; the "assassin" was because the SEALs were sometimes called upon to do assassinations. If the military needed somebody killed, we were a unit that would do it. In fact, the SEALs were surrounded by such a mystique that regular navy guys were afraid of us. There was also a lot of bullshit floating around about the SEALs, which only added to the mystique.

So when Mr. Bondi asked us if we really wanted to be pole-carrying assassins, I was still pumped from getting through the test, and I looked him in the eye and said, "Mr. Bondi, that's the only reason I joined the navy."

He just shook his head.

"Look, don't cause me any problems, just go along with everything I tell you, fold your clothes, do what you're supposed to do. I won't bother you anymore in boot camp. Because what you're gonna face . . . There's nothing I can do short of killing you that could be worse than what you're going to go through. You have no idea what the fuck you're getting into."

And he was a man of his word. From that point on in boot camp, we were never harassed or bothered or yelled at. We didn't get any of the shit they were giving to the regular boot campers. We were already elite, already separated out from the "black shoe" navy.

I met up with Mr. Bondi a few years after

that. I went to a San Diego Chargers football game one afternoon, and he was there. I walked over to him and said, "Hey, Mr. Bondi, remember me? I'm Janos! I was in your boot-camp company. I wanted to tell you I made it — I'm a Navy SEAL!" He looked at me, and his eyes grew big with fear. This was my company commander, my boot-camp instructor, and he was scared to death of me! Of course, I had been in the SEALs for about two years at that point, and I had buffed out to 220 pounds of ripped, raw navy killer. But all I wanted to do was say hello, and he was terrified! That's the mystique that the SEALs carry.

So Steve and I graduated from boot camp, and we were sent to different schools. Steve went to electronics-technician school; I went to storekeeper school. Those terms don't really mean anything if you're a SEAL; the SEALs don't have rates the way the rest of the navy does. If you're a SEAL, you're a SEAL. But in order to rise in rate, you have to have a specialty: radioman, storekeeper, electronics technician, bo'sun's mate, and so forth. So they sent us to these specialty schools before our SEAL training began. They gave us bonus points so that we could rise in rate faster. That was fair, given the extra training we were voluntarily taking on.

Steve's class went longer than mine, so I ended up going into BUD/S (Basic Underwater Demolition/SEAL) training before he did. I was class 58; he was class 59.

Was the training as tough as they'd led me to believe? It was worse. Worse than I could ever have imagined. You don't get through it if you don't want it. You have to want it. You have to want it bad. Real bad.

I left storekeeper school on a Friday and crossed the bay to Coronado to go to BUD/S. Normally, you get a couple of weeks of "pretraining," to work out and get in the swing of things before you start. But because of a quirk of timing, I got in on a Friday and started BUD/S that Monday. I had forty-eight hours to get ready.

Down by the bay there were old, dilapidated, crappy-looking World War II barracks huts. When it was time to check in, I went down to the back door of one and pounded on it. From inside, these huge, booming voices yelled out, "Who the fuck is there?"

"Storekeeper Seaman Apprentice Janos reporting for duty!"

"Get the fuck in here!"

I had just met Gunner's Mate First Class Olson, my class proctor. I handed him my stuff, and he looked it over, looked at me, and said, "Janos . . . didn't you have a brother or an uncle or something, who came through this training and quit?" My brother Jan had come through there a few years ago and had made it through. By this time he had already done one tour in Vietnam and was an old-timer. I was proud of him. So I told him, "My brother's Jan Janos, class 49, underwater demolition team 12. He graduated."

Sitting in the corner at a desk was a guy I soon came to know as "Mother" Moy. He looked up and said, "What the fuck did you say your name was?"

Olson replied, "It's another one of those stupid Janoses."

Moy looked at me and said, "Oh, yeah? You mean that puke brother of his made it? Well, I'm gonna tell you something, boy. You'd better be twice as good as that fucked-up brother of yours, and I'm gonna find out Monday."

I'm thinking, "Oh, fuck. I don't need this." The intimidation factor was huge. Of course, I realized much later they were just having fun and that they actually had a lot of respect for my brother. But I was eighteen, and I was petrified.

On Monday, the first phase of BUD/S started. SEAL training comes in three different phases. You get different drills and a different set of instructors for each phase, and you're expected to do continuously better on your run times and all your other physical exercises, even while you're being trained in new skills.

My first-phase instructor was Boatswain Mate First Class Terry "Mother" Moy. I don't have to tell you what "Mother" was short for. Nothing can compare to the fear he could strike in you. Twenty-some years later, I met him again at a SEAL reunion. By this time I had become 275-pound pro wrestler Jesse "The Body" Ventura, but when I saw him at that reunion, the hair on the back of my neck still stood up. That's how scary these guys were.

That was only the beginning of what was still to come. The first five weeks are nothing but physical training. You have to run everywhere you go. If you're moving, you're running. It's brutal. An ambulance follows you everywhere you go, and as guys go down they get whisked into it, and you probably never see them again. You can quit at any time, and most of the trainees do. The law of averages says that two out of every three will go down. An average class starts with anywhere from one hundred to one hundred and twenty guys and generally graduates between twenty and thirty-five. They had one class that graduated only four, not even a whole boat crew, which is seven guys. Mine was a summer class, and we did pretty well; we graduated with thirty-eight.

Believe it or not, the instructors aren't there to try to make you quit. Their job is to push you right to the edge. If you take yourself over the edge and quit, it's up to you. But they're not rooting for you to fail. They're rooting for you to toughen up and make it.

The first phase builds toward the fifth week, which the instructors call Motivation Week and the trainees call Hell Week. During Hell Week, the instructors divide into two groups and go on rotations: twenty-four hours on, twenty-four hours off. The trainees go with no sleep from Sunday night to Saturday morning. That's what separates the men from the boys. You're wet, you're cold, you're exhausted, you're in desperate need of sleep, and quitting starts to look awful good.

Hell Week eliminates the bananas. A banana is someone who is soft on the inside and soft on the outside, and he's out of there pretty fast. But you can never tell who will make it and who won't. Sometimes you see a guy who looks like Arnold Schwarzenegger, like he was born to do this kind of thing. Three weeks later, he's gone. You'll see another guy who looks so wimpy, it makes you wonder why he's even there. Weeks later, he's still standing. There are a lot who look soft on the outside but are hard on the inside. They survive. But you learn not to think too much about what could happen to you. You just keep working and keep getting better, faster, and stronger. There's a beach near the famous Del Coronado Hotel that has these big, sharp rock jetties. You and your class have to land rubber rafts on the rocks, coming in against huge, crashing waves. During this exercise, every class loses at least one guy to a broken leg or a dislocated shoulder, not to mention those who quit first. To make it, you have to put your fears aside and think only of the objective. One moment's hesitation is all it takes to fail.

The second phase was nine weeks of demolition and land-warfare training. We got new instructors. If you'd made it this far, the odds were good that you'd make it through the rest. At this point we learned how to patrol with weapons and how to do demolition work. The navy owns San Clemente Island, out near Catalina, home to an airstrip and some Quonset huts. On one side of the island, the regular navy shoots at targets. On the other side, SEALs learn how to blow things up. I spent two weeks out there, mostly learning how to make and detonate plastic explosives. We're not the EOD — Explosive Ordnance Division — that learns how to take apart bombs. So don't call me to dismantle a bomb, only to build one.

Those tough high-school math courses were finally coming in handy. We used the slide rule to apply mathematical equations that would tell us how much ordnance we would need to blow something up. It was critical that we get it right, because we had to carry it all. The rule of thumb was, when in doubt, overload. So after we made our calculations, we always took an extra haversack of C4 to make sure we got the job done.

The third phase of training was underwater diving, again with a whole new set of instructors. They taught us how to swim with attack boards, and how to navigate underwater at night with a compass. We learned how to dive scuba, then with mixed gas, which allowed us to dive much deeper. Then finally we learned to use an Emerson rig: pure oxygen with a rebreather that filters out the carbon dioxide and lets you reuse it so that you can dive without bubbles. The rig limits your dives to less than thirty-three feet, but it lets you dive completely undetected. No bubbles rise to the surface to give you away. You're silent and deadly.

Finally, we graduated. They give you a nice ceremony with everyone in dress uniforms and a band playing. An admiral comes by and gives you a speech. Then you have a guest speaker, usually a former SEAL, to give you an address about how you're "following a gallant force before you." I've actually spoken at one. I told the new trainees about the brotherhood they were entering into. Then you go up and get your diploma, shake the admiral's hand, and you're officially in.

That weekend after the ceremony, they gave us a lecture: "Look, you report for duty on Monday, and you've got to start out on the right foot. So don't go crazy this weekend. Don't get in trouble. And whatever you do, don't go to Tijuana!"

Back in those days, Tijuana was pretty wild and woolly. The basic rule was that if you were a gringo, you didn't walk the streets alone in Tijuana. There was a criminal element in the city that knew how to prey upon guys like us. And that's not even to mention the police force.

Well, most of the other guys listened. But

Janos the Dirty didn't. It was me and Ray Holly and Greg Platt, plus Platt's two nice-looking cousins that we latched on to just to hang out with. This was back in the times when signs on lawns in San Diego said "Dogs and Navy keep out." So it was nice to have some legitimate female companionship.

We went into the Blue Note, where Carlos Santana used to play. Platt was drunk, so he decided to take a walk to clear his head. We said, "OK, Greg, don't forget to come back!" So an hour went by, and then two. No Greg. We went back to the car. He wasn't there. We went all over the streets of Tijuana. We went back and forth across the border; we even drove all the way back to the base. Still no Greg.

In those days, Tijuana police would arrest you for nothing if you were a gringo, because it was an easy source of revenue. They knew that if you put up the money for bail, you weren't likely to bother to come back for your court date, so they got to keep it. That was their scam. Around noon each day, they'd even send around a list to all the military personnel, showing who had been arrested that night.

So along came the list, and sure enough, there was Greg's name on it. His bail was something like $150. None of us had that kind of money, so we ran back to the barracks and said, "Look, we went to Tijuana last night, and Platt's in jail." We passed the hat around and collected enough for his bail. Then we sprung him out that afternoon.

He had broken that commonsense rule: Never wander around Tijuana alone, because that's when they prey upon you. In those days, all the horror stories were true. All the guys were put in a single cell. The guards came in from time to time and sprayed them down with fire hoses, just to make life miserable for them. They were fed on cabbages that had been boiled in a garbage can. Greg said there were Americans in there, hippies, who had been in jail for months because no one had come to post their bail.

We got Greg back to the barracks in the nick of time.

On Monday we were sent to our teams. I was part of underwater demolition team 12. When you go to your team, you become known as an FNG: a Fuckin' New Guy. You're an FNG until you go on your first deployment overseas. Then when you come back, you're an old-timer. With a four-year enlistment, you do two tours of duty overseas. Normally, a tour is six months; my first was nine months, and my second was eight months.

But it seems like you're never done with training. After I graduated from BUD/S, I went to army jump school. But of course, since we were the navy elite, we went with an attitude. They expected it from us. In fact, before we left, the old-timers pulled us into a room and said, "We'd better get some bad reports on you guys, or else you'll have to answer to us." So we were on a mission: Go down there and cause as much trouble for the army as we could.

There were about twenty-five of us. When we arrived, the army tried to separate us right away. They told us, "OK, four of you are going upstairs in these barracks, two of you are going over in that barracks. . . ."

But we weren't going to accept that: "No. We're the Navy SEALs. We're going to take the top floor of these barracks. We're all going to stay together. We trust each other. We don't trust anyone else." So we walked into the top floor of the barracks and told the guys that were up there to get out. They did, without offering any resistance. That SEAL mystique comes in handy sometimes.

We were up there late that night with all the lights on, playing the radio loud, playing cards, when an army sergeant came bursting in. He was what in those days was called a shake 'n' bake: just like the chicken, fifteen minutes in the oven and they're done. He'd been to a three-week noncommissioned officer (NCO) school and had come out a sergeant. He hadn't earned it. The shake 'n' bake started yelling at us, "This is the Army Airborne School, and lights are supposed to be out at twenty-two-hundred hours! You people turn these lights out!"

We just kind of looked at him, "Who the fuck are you?"

Jim Haskell strode up to him and said, "Well, Sergeant, you got two minutes to get your ass outta here. Don't bother us. We'll shut the lights off when we feel like it." But the guy kept hollering at us, so Haskell grabbed him by the seat of the pants and tossed him out the door and into the dirt.

Needless to say, about a half hour later, we got a visit from one of the black hats. This guy was a high-ranking sergeant, an E7 or E8; he was actually one of the Airborne instructors. He cleared out all the other army guys who came into the room with him so that it was just him and us. Then he said, "Look, I know how good you guys are. I know how well-trained you are; I know the camaraderie that you have. But we have army guys here that we have to train. And we ask you for your respect."

And we did respect him. This guy was no shake 'n' bake; he was a 'Nam vet, the real deal. So we said, "No problem, Sergeant. Just a misunderstanding." Then we turned the lights off.

The actual black-hat sergeants liked us. They wanted their guys to be like us. You see, in jump school, just like in other phases of military training, they'll make you drop for push-ups. But whenever they drop one SEAL, we all drop. Where the army guys were used to getting dropped for ten push-ups, we were used to getting dropped for fifty. We could do them with one hand. That was the kind of shape we were in. When they ran in formation, we circled them. We had faced "Mother" Moy; what could jump school do to us?

The second night we were there, we snuck out and climbed up to the top of their water tower with a can of spray paint, and painted "SEAL Team One" on the side. They had to send a bunch of army guys up the next day to paint over it. We had our orders from the old-timers. We were there to cause trouble. We'd rather face the army guys than have to face the guys back on Silver Strand Beach, the navy amphibious base.

After our graduation from jump school, the same black-hat sergeant who had talked to us that first night lined everybody up, army and navy, and announced: "All army personnel are restricted to base until Monday when you leave. All navy personnel: You're due to fly out Sunday. In the meantime, get off our base." In other words, we got to go into town! They didn't want us on base causing trouble, so they restricted the army guys to their own base and sent us out! They got grounded, we got freedom!

The first thing that I did that night was grab my friend Pat Carter and tell him to put on his dress blues. Usually we went out in civilian clothes, and that's how everybody else was going out that night. But I said, "Trust me. Put on your dress blues. This is a fuckin' army town. They ain't seen no navy here." So we got into our dress blues.

We had more girls hanging around with us that night than you can possibly imagine. One woman came running out of a bar when she saw us: "I haven't seen an anchor clanker in twenty-five years!" We came back to the barracks at two in the morning, driven in by three or four girls. All our SEAL buddies saw us come in loaded down with girls. The next night, there were twenty-five navy guys out there in their dress blues!

After jump school, I went to SERE School (Survival, Escape, Resistance, and Evasion — POW School). Then I went to what is called SEAL Cadre, which is a school for advanced guerrilla warfare. At SEAL Cadre, you go out to Niland, California, and spend seven weeks doing nothing but running operations, or ops. You learn how to do everything from demolition raids to assassinations, ambushes, and kidnappings. Every guy in the unit had to learn the whole operation; everyone had to know every facet, including how to lead an op. At that time, we did it all in the context of jungle warfare, because our mission was Vietnam.

One night we were out running ops on a river. There were two crews of us, and we were supposed to "blow up" two bridges on this river that none of us had ever been on before. As we were making our way down the river in pitch-blackness, we started to notice a sound that kept getting louder and louder. It sounded like rushing water. By the time we realized what it was, it was too late to do anything about it. In the dark, we couldn't make out the huge dam that lay right in front of us until we were going over it.

Rick Dees, in the front of the boat, managed to grab on to something to keep from going over. He got to shore and signaled the other boat to let them know what was happening. They saw him and made it safely to shore. I was already over the edge and falling. I tried to grab on to the wall of the dam, but I couldn't get a hold on anything. I got a brief, crazy vision of myself as a cat in a cartoon, leaving claw marks all the way down.

I fell to the bottom of the dam and landed in a huge, churning mass of white water. The current was so strong it tossed me around and around like I was a pebble in a washing machine. It just kept spinning me around and sucking me down, and wouldn't let me up for air. There was absolutely nothing I could do. I was helpless against the water's power. As I think about it now, I can still feel how my lungs burned from holding my breath.

As my body was lurching and reeling under the swirling current, I started to accept that I was going to die. I was trying to decide whether I'd rather let my breath out and drown or just keep holding it until I passed out. I decided I'd rather just hold my breath. Once I'd made up my mind how I was going to die, I started feeling sorry for my mom and dad. I had a very clear vision of the two of them bending over my casket, crying. Then, suddenly, my feet scraped the river bottom, and I shot up to the surface. After a few breaths, I broke clear of the washing-machine effect at the foot of the dam. I was the last one out of the water and the longest one under.

That was the first time I really began to think that there was a force guiding my life that was bigger than coincidence. One of us should have died on the river that night. Statistically, somebody shouldn't have made it. If you think about where I ended up after I got to the bottom of that dam, it really should have been me. But for whatever reason, I lived. It made me think.

That accident should never have happened. In a real ops situation, there would have been reconnaissance done on that entire river area, and we would have been told about the dam. Somebody screwed up, and it almost cost me my life. Later, they tried to send a dive team in to retrieve our weapons, but they had to pull out because the current was too strong. Our weapons are probably still at the bottom of that dam.

There finally came a time when all the training was done. I graduated from SEAL Cadre on a Wednesday, and the following Monday morning I was scheduled to be deployed overseas. I had hardly more than a weekend before I would find out what it was like to put my training to use in a real-life war. So, of course, I quickly came up with a productive way to fill the time. My buddy Ray Holly took me aside and said, "You know what we oughtta do? We oughtta go to Reno, Nevada. Prostitution is legal there."

I didn't believe him at first, but he swore he wasn't kidding. So we flew out there, hooked up with a buddy, and rented a car. We started out trying to gamble in the casinos at Tahoe, but as soon as we started winning, they checked our IDs, found out we weren't twenty-one, and kicked us out. They wouldn't even let us have the money we'd won. So we thought, "What the hell. Let's go check out the ranches."

Now remember, I was really still just a kid. I was still five years away from meeting Terry and getting married. This was all new to me. I hadn't been overseas yet. We were scheduled to be deployed to a part of the world where there was a war going on. For all I knew, I could be dead pretty soon, so I wanted to have as much fun and do as much living as possible while I still could. This was long before AIDS, before casual sex could mean death.

The Starlight Ranch and the Moonlight Ranch were out in the middle of the desert. You pull up to this gate alongside a huge cyclone fence topped with barbed wire. There's an intercom there, and you hit the buzzer. The madam answers, and if you can convince her you're not with the Hell's Angels, she'll buzz you in.

So we were buzzed in, and we walked into the parlor. The madam said, "Girls, we have visitors." Out came six or eight girls who looked just like *Playboy* playmates. Incredible. You go down the line, they each tell you their name, and you pick out the one you want. In those days it was cheap — ten to fifteen bucks. So we each picked out a lady and did our thing, then we went back to town and catted around a while. Then, early the next morning, we decided to go to another ranch.

At this second ranch, I picked out one girl because she was wearing these cool-looking rectangular hippie glasses. I don't remember her name. But as we went back into the room, she couldn't take her eyes off my belt. At SEAL Cadre, we'd been shooting Stoner machine guns. In the evenings I had linked together about twenty feet of empty shell casements and was wearing some of them as a belt around my jeans. She said, "I want that belt."

I grinned at her. "Oh yeah?"

"What'll it take?" she asked. "How much

do you want for it?"

I didn't tell her I had twenty more feet back in the barracks, and could make a dozen more belts just like it anytime I wanted. "Why don't you make me an offer?"

She said, "Well, how about a trick and ten dollars?" I'm probably one of the only people in the world who's gone into a Nevada ranch and been paid. I used that ten dollars to go to another one.

Afterward, I asked her the same question she probably got from every guy: how a nice girl got to be doing what she was doing. She said, "I love sex. Plus, I can make ten times here what I could make anywhere else. I can retire in a few years." When she found out that I was about to go overseas, she gave me her business card and told me to write to her if I ever got lonely.

We kept in touch my first trip overseas. I'd get a letter from her saying, "Dear Jim, I'm writing to you between tricks . . ." Whenever I got a letter from her, I held it up for the guys to see and said, "Hey! I got a letter from my Nevada hooker!" When I told her I was planning to buy a Harley-Davidson when I got back from overseas, she wrote, "Come by and pick me up. We'll take off for a while." But I never did. By the time I got back to the States, I'd lost track of her. I kind of regret that. I never saw her again.

On Monday, we were shipped overseas. We spent a few days on a god-awful flight that I could handle only because I was nineteen and didn't know what I was getting myself into. We finally got into the base at Subic in the Philippines, got assigned to our platoons, and were scattered to the four winds.

I spent a total of seventeen months in Southeast Asia during my two tours. I spent time in Vietnam, Hong Kong, Korea, Thailand, Okinawa, Guam, and the Philippines. I was lucky, though. I got in at the tail end of the war. We were already in withdrawal mode by the time I got there, so there wasn't much to do. We were already facing what they were calling "peace with honor." We did a bit of surveillance and reconnaissance work in case the marines were called in. They mainly used us as a bargaining chip to get the Vietnamese to the negotiating table.

I loved being overseas for one reason: I was an adult there. Back home, I was still considered a child: In most places I couldn't walk into a bar and buy a drink; I couldn't even vote. I consider that a great hypocrisy, that I could be required to die for my country, but my country wouldn't even show me the respect of treating me as an adult. That double standard was what caused the hippie rebellion: the hypocrisy that forced kids to go die in a war when those same kids weren't even allowed to vote against the people who sent them over there.

One of the most traumatic things I ever faced was coming back from nine months overseas. I had been back five days, and I went in to my executive officer, Lieutenant Commander Bruce Dyer, and requested to be sent overseas again. He told me, "You can't. You've got to be stateside for at least nine months. And why on earth would you want to go back?"

I said, "Because over there I'm an adult. Over there I'm treated like an adult; no one's questioning me. Over here, I'm a child. I'd rather be back over there."

I loved the Philippines. I was stationed at Subic, and I loved going into Olongapo. It was more like the Wild West than any other place on Earth. In Olongapo, there's a one-mile stretch of road that has 350 bars and 10,000 girls on it every night. Think what that meant to a nineteen-year-old navy guy! At various bars you had your pick of rock 'n' roll, country and western, you name it. There was one bar that was nothing but transvestites. It was a decadent city. To the kid I was then, it was paradise.

Anything went in Olongapo. The SEALs have a proud tradition of doing without the unnecessary conveniences in life such as underwear. On any given night at a bar in Olongapo, one of us might hop up on a table and yell, "Skivvy check!" We'd all jump up and drop our trousers to prove we weren't wearing any. To this day, I still honor that tradition most of the time. The day I was sworn in as governor, there was some concern that someone might yell for a skivvy check in the middle of my inaugural speech.

The value system was so different overseas that when I came back stateside, I had a difficult time relating to American women. When a girl went with you in Olongapo, there was no question about what you were going to do. In the States, you had to wine 'em and dine 'em. At that point in my life, I was barely out of my teens; I wasn't into wining and dining. The libido was still in charge. A lot of my buddies felt that way too. Many of them got around the awkwardness they felt with American women by marrying Filipino girls.

It truly was like the frontier. They warned us never to get into a vehicle unless we were with another American. I usually stuck to that rule, but there was one night when I was drunk, stranded, and trying to get back to base. I flagged down a jeepney (a converted World War II jeep, many of which were decorated with tassels and religious icons) and was glad to see that although there were three or four Filipinos inside, there was also one American guy. I got in, but I dozed off along the way. The next thing I knew, the American guy was gone, and the Filipinos had all drawn knives and were demanding my watch.

Now, this wasn't just an ordinary watch. This was a custom Rolex Submariner waterproof dive watch with the SEAL trident on it. We all had these watches, and we wore them as a symbol of our unity. I was looking at a choice between death and giving up that watch, and I had a split second to think. I did a nosedive out of the moving jeepney, landed parachute-style on the ground, and rolled into the bushes. I had to walk the rest of the way back to Subic, but I kept my watch.

But that was why we loved it. It was wild, decadent, unpredictable. In one bar, they had a pond with a live alligator. For a peso, you could buy a baby duck to feed to it. One night I was out with my friend George Hudak, and we were drunker than hell. He bought one of the ducks and said, "To hell with feeding the alligator!" He popped the baby duck into his own mouth. He was missing a tooth in front, and I could see one little webbed foot flailing around in the gap between his teeth.

This is the kind of thing you get when you live life on the edge. A SEAL will defy death at least twice a week, whether it's jumping out of an airplane, rappelling out of a helicopter, or swimming through the water at night with explosives strapped to his back. When you get that kind of familiarity with death, barriers go down. The things you're expected to do in combat situations are so far beyond the pale, anything less seems insignificant.

I don't like what happened later in the navy's Tailhook scandal; I think what those officers did was wrong. But I understand why it happened. When you get a force of that many hundreds of warriors together, there's bound to be trouble. We're responsible for making them what they are. You just can't bring them back into civilization and expect that everything that was drilled into them is going to go away.

When you're dealing with death face-to-face, there are no rules. It's all about survival. After that, bad behavior doesn't affect you all that much. If the public thought Tailhook was bad, imagine what they'd think of any given night in Olongapo! That's the mistake those young officers made: They brought Olongapo back with them to Las Vegas, and it got out of hand.

War isn't civilized. War is failure. It's the ultimate result of a breakdown in public policy, and soldiers are the machines that handle that breakdown. In warfare, you're taught to do whatever you have to to stay alive. Can you imagine bringing that mind-set into a party?

When you become a SEAL, you have to accept the fact that eventually your job might require you to take a life. How do you justify that? It goes against everything you're taught. It goes against all religion. It goes against all common sense. When you put yourself so far beyond all things civilized that you're prepared to kill, how serious does it seem to grab a woman by her breasts?

When Demi Moore was doing the movie *G.I. Jane*, about the first woman to become a Navy SEAL, she wanted to come to one of our reunions to see what it was like. But when she actually got there and was face-to-face with the real thing, she was scared to death. They messed with her, just to shock her. One of them yelled, "Hey, Demi! This movie better be good, or we're gonna hunt you down!"

131

They reacted that way because she was going to portray herself as one of us, even though she'd never been through BUD/S; she'd never done the things the rest of us had done to earn our trident. In effect, they were saying to her, "You wanna dance to the music, let's see if you can pay the fiddler." We're a proud organization. If anyone tries to pretend they're a SEAL, God help them. You have to earn the right to be a SEAL warrior.

I don't talk about what I did over there. I never have yet, to anybody. Because when we returned from overseas after my first deployment, we were brought into a room by my commanding officer, Lieutenant Commander Robert Peterson, and he gave us direct orders never to talk about what we had seen and done over there. This was right at the time of the My Lai massacre trial, when the press was trying to dig up whatever they could from anyone who had been there. I've held to that order all these years. I stuck with it when questions about my Vietnam experience were raised during my campaign, and I will continue to honor it. Once a SEAL, always a SEAL.

CHAPTER 5

"THE BODY"

My second tour of duty overseas was quieter than my first. By then the war was over for the SEALs, so I was sent straight back to the Philippines just in case things started up again. There was nothing to do except to stay in practice and to have fun. Sad to say, any time a war ends, the military suddenly turns chickenshit. The military is really only at its best when it has a mission. Without a war to keep them occupied, the various branches of the military all have a tendency to get more and more obsessive about boot polishing and hair length. When my second tour was done, I decided I was done with the navy.

I was never tempted to make a career out of the navy, even though at that time they were offering SEALs $10,000 bonuses to stay in. That was a pretty big chunk of cash to stick in your pocket, especially in 1973. When I got back stateside, Bruce Dyer, my executive officer, called me into his office and said, "Well, Janos. You're a good operator. What'll it take to keep you in?"

I said, "You want the truth, Mr. Dyer? Fifty thousand and the rank of commander." I wanted to be one higher than him.

He said, "You can't get that!"

And I said, "You asked!" What's amazing is that today I'm a two-star admiral! That's the rank the navy gave me for my victory as governor. Bruce Dyer was here for my inauguration. He had to salute me.

I was waiting for my official discharge from the navy to come through. I still hadn't set a particular course for my life. My plans only extended as far as buying a Harley and traveling around California. So for a while I lived free and easy and became a part of the incredible scene that was the early seventies in America.

Believe it or not, even while I was a SEAL, I had participated in the peace movement. I marched at peace rallies. I admit it wasn't so much because of my great love of peace as it was because of my great love of female companionship. To the women in the movement, I was the poor beleaguered victim of the system, sent off against his will to fight this horrible war. They didn't realize the navy had no draft!

I loved the braless thing. I'm very heterosexual. I'd see women out burning their bras, and I'd go over with a lighter, "Can I help?" I did participate seriously, though, in the antidraft movement. To this day, I'm against the draft. I believe that the military is much stronger if it's an all-volunteer organization.

In San Diego and Coronado, I met up with some local bikers, the Mongols. Soon after, I started riding and hanging out with them. While I was still waiting for my official discharge, I decided to become a "prospect," a candidate for Mongols membership. Prospecting is a little like BUD/S. You become a gofer, and the full-fledged members go out of their way to mess with you. They'd make you do push-ups. But after what I'd been through in the SEALs, this was nothing. I could do push-ups all day.

It was a new adventure. I'd ride onto base on my Harley, wearing my colors, then take them off and get into my navy uniform. Then at the end of the day, I'd take off my navy uniform and put it in a locker, put on my colors, and ride off on my Harley.

I was into the biker mystique and the biker lifestyle. I loved riding Harleys. In those days, when you bought your first Harley, you also got a pair of what they called "Originals" — Levi's jeans. From the day you first put them on, you never wash them. After a while, they got so covered in oil and stuff that on hot summer days the oil would turn to liquid again and come off on my hands. I still have that same pair, still unwashed, in the garage.

The president of the Mongols was a huge, big Mexican named James "Fatman" Rivera. Many bikers have big potbellies. They aren't exactly the cleanest guys on the planet. We were the largest club in Southern California, bigger than Hell's Angels. We were 90 percent Mexican. I was one of the few white guys who could ride into East L.A. and not be bothered, because of the patch I wore on my back. I was a gringo, but they figured I must be OK if I rode with the Mongols. I've always had a thing for dark-haired women. Terry has dark hair. The Asian women I met in Olongapo had dark hair. And the Mexican women I met when I was riding had dark hair. Being accepted in that community had its advantages.

Technically, you might call the Mongols a gang, but that word gives the wrong impression. The biker mystique was mostly created by the movies, and the bikers started trying to live up to the image. Everyone assumed we rode around and took over little towns, like Marlon Brando did in *The Wild Ones*.

Mostly, we were about riding Harleys and enjoying the freedom of life on the road. We wanted to be left to ourselves. We didn't want trouble. If anyone messed with us, we would defend ourselves; we didn't take shit from anybody. But we had a lifestyle, and we just wanted to be left alone to enjoy it. We weren't looking for trouble. Unfortunately, trouble sometimes has a way of following you.

We used to ride onto an Indian reservation, slip the chief a few bucks, and throw a party on Indian land. The cops couldn't do anything to us because we were inside the borders of a sovereign nation. They'd sit on the highway and watch, but they couldn't touch us.

I didn't stay in the Mongols long, but I rose to prominence quickly. I was hard-core to begin with, and they respected me for being a SEAL. When I was voted in, I became sergeant at arms, which was third in command of our chapter. But eventually, after I got my patch and became a full member, I started to see that it was a dead-end trip. I wanted to do more with my life. There were guys in the club, forty, fifty years old, who really had nothing but their Harleys. They lived in crappy little houses, and their only ambition in life was to have the best-looking Harley. I wanted more out of life than that. So I rode with the club for only about nine months, then I came home to Minnesota and started college.

I enrolled in North Hennepin Community College as a twenty-three-year-old freshman on the GI bill. I really didn't know what I wanted to take at the time, and I really didn't care, so I didn't waste time and money going to a university. I had a vision of playing pro football. I figured if I started out playing at a community college, I could get a scholarship and go on to a university from there.

It was at North Hennepin that I made my acting debut. They were putting on Aristophanes' play *The Birds* that semester, and one day while I was working out in the weight room, the instructor, Don Duran, came in, looking to cast the part of Hercules. He looked at me and decided I would be perfect, so he recruited me. It was fun, watching it go from all of us standing on the stage reading lines, to the full, polished production that sold out the four nights that it played in the auditorium. I went back there for a visit about two weeks before the inauguration, and they had me autograph the stage.

I also took introduction to theater and beginning acting; I had fun with it. But this was not yet the start of my Hollywood career, because by that time I had seen "Superstar" Billy Graham, and I had figured out what I wanted to do with my life. I took the acting classes because I knew they'd come in handy for my new career as a professional wrestler.

Wrestling is theater. I've always referred to wrestling as "ballet with violence." It's got drama, just like the shows you go to see onstage. But saying it's "theater" is not the same thing as saying it's fake. The "ballet" part is that maybe some of the moves are staged, choreographed, planned in advance, but the violence is real. I know; I've felt it. And feeling is believing. There's no acting training in the world that can teach you to wrestle pain-free.

I studied hard all that semester, even while I was training for wrestling. I started out the semester with a solid 4.0, straight As. But then I met Terry, and my 4.0 took a nosedive down to a 3.3. See what women do to you? They ruin all your good intentions! (Joke.)

While I was going to college, I got a job as a nightclub doorman, which is a polite term for a bouncer. On Thursday nights they'd have that sexist institution known as Ladies'

Night, where women got to go in and drink cheap. The bar owners knew that if they could entice the women in there with half-price drinks, they would soon be followed by a bevy of thirsty guys.

At that point, I was still having a tough time relating to American women. Life in Southeast Asia was so different, it was hard to readapt to a whole other set of rules. I wasn't doing well on the dating scene with Minnesota girls.

I was working the door that night along with two cops. Terry walked in, and our eyes met. Her eyes were so beautiful. A feeling came over me, and I had to meet this woman; I had to know who she was. She showed her ID to one of the cops at the door, and then she headed toward me. As she approached, I was thinking, "God, what do I say? I've got to say something to her, I can't just let her walk on by." So I said, "Can I see your ID please?"

She said, "But I just showed him."

I said, "I don't care how old you are, I just want to know your name." That was my line. But instead of just telling me her name, she went all through her purse and pulled out her ID again. Later, though, she admitted she'd felt the same way about me when our eyes first locked across the room.

At that time I was already evolving into "The Body." I'd never gotten the chance to be a hippie, so the first thing I did when I got out of the navy was grow my hair down to my shoulders and bleach it blond. I was already pumping iron like a madman and training hard for wrestling, so my body was bulking out. I was working out three nights a week at the Seventh Street Gym at Seventh and Hennepin Avenue with an ex–pro wrestler named Eddie Sharkey. With the bleached blond hair I looked a good bit like my hero, "Superstar" Billy Graham, who was really hot then, so I was cultivating that look for myself. I'd decided that if I was going to get into wrestling, I was going for it with all I had.

That night, when Terry and I sat down and started talking, the first thing she said to me was, "God! You look just like 'Superstar' Billy Graham!" That's how I found out that Terry always watched wrestling on TV before she went out on Saturday nights.

"I ought to," I said, devil that I am, "he's my older brother." I had to say something.

Actually, it turned out that she hated him. Graham was a villain, and he was always bragging. But we got talking about wrestling. She remembered when she used to watch wrestling with her dad as a kid. Here I had something in common with this beautiful woman, and it just happened to be wrestling, my new passion.

She excused herself, went over to the friends she'd come in with, and told them, "You're not going to see much of me tonight. I've got to talk more with that guy over there at the door." We talked all night. It was love at first sight. Although, it's not really true that you can have love at first sight. Love comes later. But you can have lust at first sight; or at least I know I can. We definitely fell in lust that night.

I got her phone number and called her the next day to invite her out on a date. I took her to a place we South Siders called the Yacht Club. It was actually a quiet little neighborhood bar called the Schooner. It was the kind of place where you could chew tobacco and spit on the floor. That worked for me, because I'd taken up chewing tobacco while I was in the service. My dad had even gone there when he was working. I wanted to take Terry to meet some of the South Siders who hung out there, so I had worked hard to convince her that it was a nice, quiet, safe place right across from the Third Precinct police station.

I picked her up and brought her to the Schooner that night. We weren't in there for more than ten or fifteen minutes when three or four huge cops burst in the door, yanked this guy off a bar stool, and started dragging him toward the door. He resisted, and they beat the shit out of him right in front of our eyes and hauled him away. It turned out he deserved it: He'd been roughing up his girlfriend in the parking lot, and she'd walked across the street to the precinct and filed charges on him. Quiet neighborhood bar. Yeah.

That was our first date. Believe it or not, she agreed to go with me on a second one. That time we went to the movies. Unfortunately, she let me pick the movie. Terry and I do have our differences, especially when it comes to movies. Even knowing her the short time I had, and especially given the fact that we were on a date, I should have guessed that she'd have been happier to see something like Ryan O'Neal in *Love Story*. Instead I took her to see Charles Bronson in *Death Wish*.

Even after that, she still wanted to keep seeing me. We started dating a lot and got deeply involved. At first, the other guys resented her a little, because I had always hung out with them in my spare time and now Terry was taking priority over them. I was the first of the South Siders to have a serious relationship. If you'd have told them back in high school, back before I won that first bet on New Year's Eve, that I'd be the first to have a serious girlfriend, none of them would have believed it. Imagine what they'd have thought if they found out I'd be the first one to get married, too.

About that time, I was finishing my training as a wrestler and was sending out pictures to different promoters around the country. I got a call from Kansas City, Missouri, from the promoter Bob Geigel. Eddie Sharkey had talked to him earlier and told him, "I got you a kid here that I think has the potential to be a great wrestler." When Geigel asked me to come down for a tryout, I jumped in my car, said good-bye to Terry, and headed down to Kansas City. I had a beautiful girlfriend back home, two hundred dollars in my pocket, a Chevy with a dented front fender, and no idea what I was getting myself into.

I was down there for a couple of months, and I really missed Terry. She came down to visit me once, and she cried when she saw how I was living. I was staying in a twenty-three-dollar-a-week hotel; I guess it was what you would call a flophouse. It didn't bother me. I'd lived in worse when I was in the service. But I missed her even more after she left. I knew that I loved her, and I wanted to spend the rest of my life with her. I just knew it. But being the typical noncommittal bachelor that I was, at first I just asked her to come down and live with me. She had a job and her own apartment; she was very self-sufficient, and she said, "I ain't leavin' up here unless I get a bigger commitment than 'come on down and live with me.' " So, over the phone, I said, "Well, I guess I'll just have to say 'Will you marry me?' " And she started crying and said yes.

We set up the whole wedding over the phone, and when it was time, I came home from wrestling for a week. Terry's mom tried to talk her out of it; she didn't want to see her giving up her independence so soon. She was only nineteen. But Terry has always said she was sure. She said she knew that this guy was going places, and she knew for sure she wanted to go on that journey.

Even on the day of the wedding, Terry's mom was still trying to talk her into putting it off. But my mom was all for it. Terry had gotten close to my mom during the time that I was gone, while we were having our whirlwind courtship over the phone. She ended up being closer to my mom, in some ways, than I ever was.

Terry and I actually knew each other for

only nine months before we got married. We were married in a little place called Timothy Lutheran Church in Saint Louis Park, a suburb of Minneapolis. Terry had made all the arrangements, sent out all the invitations, and handled just about everything except the date. I had promised myself that I wouldn't get married before I was twenty-four, so I made sure our wedding date was set for July 18, 1975: three days after my twenty-fourth birthday.

The prime directive of wrestling is to protect your opponent as you would protect yourself. It's their living, just as it's yours. You have to learn to make the match as realistic as possible without doing real harm. Those body slams and turnbuckles — where the ropes are connected to the corner ring posts — they jar you, they bump you around, they certainly don't feel real nice. But it's your opponent's responsibility to make sure that nothing that he does to you is going to cause you an injury, and it's your responsibility to do the same for him.

So how do you make sure, when you're slamming somebody with a folding chair for example, that you're not going to injure him? Make sure he's flat. Make sure you're not hitting any vital parts. This is what you

146

go through seven months of training to learn how to do. None of what you see is staged or rehearsed — it's all spontaneous — but the technique behind it all is an art form that requires careful discipline.

But that in no way means that it's fake. When someone body-slams you, they won't injure you if they're doing it right, but, rest assured, you feel it! When you're in wrestling, you're in pain so often you learn to take it for granted. I've always said feeling is believing. If you think wrestling is fake, get in the ring and let a professional wrestler body-slam you a couple of times!

It's very much like dancing, like doing a waltz. Where in dancing it's the man who leads, in wrestling it's the bad guy who leads. The "heel," as he used to be called, is the one who is driving the match. Back then, you were either a heel or a babyface. Today it's different — today everyone's a personality — but back then you were clearly one or the other. That was the shtick: It was a battle of good versus evil, babyface against heel. I was very certain from the beginning where I fit into the scheme of things: I wanted to be a heel.

You get a lot more creative opportunities as the bad guy. There are more challenges. You're responsible for working up the audience, so you get out there and yell and scream and interact with them — far more than the babyface ever does. But one big reason I wanted to be the bad guy was because of that rebellious streak in me. I always rooted for the bad guy when I was a fan cheering "Superstar" Billy Graham just because it was what you weren't supposed to do. The heels have their fans, too.

You establish yourself as a heel by taking on a persona that everybody can have fun hating. I knew that everybody hated beach bums; they figured that beach bums spent their lives doing nothing but hanging out in the surf, getting tans, and chasing women. So I kept my bleached blond hair, wore outrageous sunglasses, earrings, and the big feather boas that later became my trademark. Then I named myself after a highway in California.

You also let the fans know you're a bad guy by playing dirty. You cheat whenever you can, the more outrageously the better. You're arrogant and boastful, you never tell the truth, and at the end of the match, no matter how things go, you always scream to the crowd that you've been ripped off. Or you use the old standby: hollering that the referee is biased against you and is sabotaging the match.

Typically, you'd fight somebody three times in a row or more and build up the hostility between the two of you. The babyface almost always prevailed, though it was the promoter who made that call. As a bad guy, it was usually my job to lose. But even though I'd lose the match, I still won, because I drew people in. The fans loved to hate me. And they had pretty short memories — even when I lost, I'd be back next week and nobody would even remember what had happened the last time.

My strength was in working the crowds — I was good with the psychological stuff. If you could get the crowds involved, the job was that much easier to do. I'd wait until the referee's back was turned, and then I'd pull my opponent's hair. The fans would start squealing, "He pulled his hair! He pulled his hair!" And I'd yell back, "Shaddap!" Of course, the referee could call only what he saw. It really was a three-way endeavor, because the referee had to be sure to turn his back every once in a while to give me the opportunity to pull my dirty tricks. That's called building up your heat.

It's very much a performing art, only with violence. You work on a dramatic build. You have moments when you build and moments when you settle back in, but if you and your opponent are really working well off each other, the two of you eventually build toward what's called a peak. Then you go into the finish. Usually the match ended either when the babyface pinned the heel or, more likely, when the heel did something to get disqualified so that he didn't have to risk getting pinned.

If I had told you about all this twenty years ago, I would have gotten myself in a world of hurt. I can only tell you this now because wrestling has pretty much been exposed, and the rules have changed. Everyone today knows it's a show. Back then, though, there were unwritten laws within the business that kept you from letting any outsider in on how it was all done. If somebody called you a fake, it was considered an insult to your professional pride, and you'd probably hit them. This was way before the heyday of the personal-injury lawsuit.

In those days you didn't get a guaranteed salary or fee. You were paid a percentage of the gate, so if you wanted to work and get paid, you had to prove to the promoters that you were a draw. Early in my career, I once wrestled sixty-three nights straight. But to really be a draw and make the money, you not only had to be great in the ring, you also had to be a tremendous talker when they handed you that microphone for the TV interviews. You had to make people hate you. You had to have a talent for irritating people. I did.

But I wasn't one of the real bad guys in the wrestling business: The promoters had that market cornered. They'd tell you when to wrestle, where to wrestle, what moves to use, and whether you were going to win or lose, but at the same time they'd also call you an independent contractor so you'd have to pay self-employment tax. What's "independent" about that? It was a fraud, a lie. We were employees, but we got no benefits. They had no loyalty to you either. Once you stopped bringing in the crowds, you were out of there. They wouldn't give you a second thought.

After seven months of working out with former pro wrestler Eddie Sharkey at the Seventh Street Gym, and learning the ropes, I got the opportunity from promoters Bob Geigel, Gust Karras, and Pat O'Connor — the former world champ — for my first pro match. They called me back down to Kansas City and worked me in the ring with O'Connor for a couple of weeks until I had run out of money. They do that on purpose, because if you're broke they know they have you. They know you'll do anything they want you to do.

When I started wrestling, there were twenty-six different territories, with regionalized TV. You'd wrestle in one territory until you weren't drawing in money, then you'd move to another territory. In the next territory, you'd be all new again, because there wasn't national coverage like there is today. Lord Alfred Hayes, a popular local wrestler, was headed for a new part of the country. He had asked for a few days off to pack, so I was going to be filling in for him.

The first night I got into the pro ring was at Century II Auditorium in Wichita. I was going to be fighting a veteran babyface named Omar Atlas. When I arrived backstage, I could already hear the crowd getting rowdy. All the eyes, all the lights, all the focus was on that big square of light framed in ropes in the middle of the auditorium, where in a few minutes I was going to climb in and voluntarily get the shit pounded out of me.

Bob Geigel took me aside in a back room and said, "You know, kid, nobody wins their first match."

I said, "I know."

Bob called Omar into the room and told him, "This is the kid's first match. Take care of him out there."

Since it was my first match ever, Omar was to call the match more than I would, even though I was the bad guy. Bob told him, "If the match is the shits, hit him with two dropkicks, cover him, and beat him. But if you think the match is goin' good, let him throw you out over the top rope."

Throwing someone out over the top rope in those days was an automatic disqualification, but it was something the heel might do in desperation if he was getting the crap kicked out of him. He would throw the babyface over the ropes and out of the ring. He gets himself disqualified that way and loses the match, but he doesn't get pinned. If you have to lose — and I did — your best odds are to lose in the showiest way possible. It was completely up to Omar. If he wanted to, he could finish me with two dropkicks.

I went in there and gave it all I had. I strutted out there, the world's biggest braggart. I made fun of Omar, and when the crowd booed me, I climbed up on the ropes and insulted them. Did they hate me! Whenever I did something rotten to Omar, the crowd went nuts.

Finally it was time to "go home" for the finish. Omar and I were squared off in the ring. Lucky for me, Omar was a great guy and didn't have a big ego. He knew the match was a huge success, and he knew I was going places. So he decided to give me a great finale. He gave me a little knowing smile and whispered, "Amigo, throw me out over the top." I picked Omar up and tossed him out over the ropes. He landed with a heavy thud and immediately started "selling" the crowd, playing hurt. I paraded around the ring while they booed me like hell.

The promoters knew they had a winner. Later that night, Bob Geigel came up to me and said, "This is your first match? You look better'n some guys who've been eight or nine years out there!"

Coincidentally, the last match of my career, in Winnipeg in the spring of 1986 against Tony Atlas, ended the same way, with me getting disqualified. I began and ended with an Atlas and a disqualification. It was a nice, poetic way to end my career.

"The Body" caught on pretty fast after that. I developed a reputation for being outrageous, badder than bad. I had a talent for interacting with the fans. If you're successful as a bad guy, you know nobody handed it to you. It's up to you to draw the crowds, to develop the hatred. All the good guy has to do is stand for Mom, apple pie, and the girl back home. As the bad guy, you have to draw out a response. You have to make them hate you.

And back then, the fans truly hated the bad guys. You worked them into such frenzies that they really believed you were what you were in the ring. That's another reason why I went by Jesse "The Body" Ventura, to protect myself and my family. It worked out well, because then I could have my phone number in my own name, and the fans had no way of knowing my real name was James Janos. It kept a cushion between the fans and my family. I didn't take my family to matches often, because it was dangerous for them. One time I brought Terry to a match, and the crowd started pelting both of us with snow cones. Also, you really don't need for your kids to see all these people screaming insults and throwing things at their dad. Terry, Tyrel, and Jade went by the last name Janos for years, up until 1984, when the World Wrestling Federation went national, exposed everything, and changed the whole business of wrestling from a spectacle of good guy against bad to a contest of personalities.

But until then, I had a fair number of run-ins with angry fans. One night in Sioux Falls around 1979 or 1980, I was in my dressing room after the match, and I heard this angry mob gathering outside the door. I'd done something rotten and beaten their favorite babyface, so they were out for my hide. I just stood there not knowing what to do, while the security guards were trying to get the crowd under control. All of a sudden, the door split in half — ka-BOOM! The top half of the door came sliding into the room. I looked out over the splintered remains of the door and saw what looked to be half of the Sioux Falls police department, out there in the middle of the melee with nightsticks, pounding away at these people, trying to keep them from beating the snot out of me.

I got the occasional death threat. I never took them seriously, because I figure the ones you have to watch out for are the ones that don't warn you in advance. And besides, back then the heels got a police escort back to their dressing rooms every night.

There was a guy one night in Eugene, Oregon, who tried to kill me. I don't remember who I was wrestling or how the match went. At the end of it, as the police were taking me back to my dressing room, a fight broke out at ringside. I figured they were needed more back there, and with the focus out on the fight I thought I'd be safe going the rest of the way by myself, so I turned the cops loose.

They disappeared, and I was alone. I thought I was safe. But all of a sudden, from around the back of the bleachers, came this young kid with a wild look in his eye. I recognized him from earlier that night. He'd been shouting something at me, and I'd told him to shut up — or probably something a lot worse than that. And now he was coming at me. He looked at me with cold hatred and growled, "Ventura, I'm gonna stick this up your ass."

Then he reached behind him and pulled out a wicked hunting knife with a ten-inch blade.

You can read in a guy's eyes whether or not he has serious intent. This guy wasn't sloppy, out-of-control mad; he was white with rage, but very calm. There was no doubt in my mind he was prepared to hurt me.

I was standing there in nothing but tights — a few thin strands of nylon away from being totally naked. I was completely on my own, but the SEAL training was kicking in. I was calculating how I was going to defend myself. I knew that without even so much as a towel to use as defense, I'd probably have to sacrifice something. I would most likely have to give him my arm before I could take him down.

But all of a sudden, somebody dropped silently out of the bleachers, rushed up behind the guy, spun him around, and handcuffed him. It turned out he was a plainclothes cop who had taken his kid to the matches that night. He just happened to look down at that moment and saw this guy coming at me with the knife.

That officer did an outstanding job. I thanked him even though, of course, they could do nothing to the guy because he was only sixteen years old. All they could do was release him to the custody of his parents.

That wasn't the only time I've been assaulted — and the next time the perpetrator definitely wasn't a minor. I was wrestling Tito Santana in Denver. Those matches were great because the crowds were heavily Latino, and they really hated me for what I did to Tito. In one match, Tito had thrown me out of the ring, and I was standing there beefing and whining and putting on a show. All of a sudden, I got this searing pain down the whole length of my spine. I spun around, ready to deck whoever did it. Standing there was this old lady, dripping in diamonds, with these long, long fingernails. This wealthy senior citizen had taken those nails and raked them down my back with all her strength. She drew blood; she had literally carved me open. I didn't deck her, but I did tell the cops to arrest her. And they did. She was charged with assault, at the age of seventy.

But there were fans on the other end of the spectrum, too. There were rebellious young college kids who, just like I did when I was their age, rooted for the bad guy because it was the obnoxious thing to do. In fact, I once wrestled in a place where the entire crowd was rooting for me: Lino Lakes Prison. Prison crowds always cheer the bad guy and boo the good guy, but I was going to hedge my bet a little. Before the match, I went out and bought several cartons of cigarettes. I went into the ring that night and tossed them out to the inmates. I couldn't have been more popular with them if I'd been tossing out gold.

I'd endeared myself to them. So that night, I had some help getting away with my dirty tricks! The referee would come stomping up to me and say, "Did you pull his hair?" I'd say, "No I didn't — ask them!" And all the inmates would scream back "Noooooo!"

I enjoyed the support I got that night, but in spite of all the fun I had it was a little eerie to be going inside a prison. When I walked in and heard those doors clank closed behind me, I got a chill up the back of my neck. It was awfully nice to be let back out again at the end of the night.

It was worth it, though, because I could see I'd really brightened their days. They had a great time and they appreciated the fact that I'd come there to give them a show. To be perfectly honest, they behaved themselves better than a lot of the people I usually encountered out in the auditoriums.

Not all of the misbehavior came from the fans. I encountered it in the ring once, too. It was a tag-team match in Portland, Oregon, with me and Bull Ramos against Johnny Boyd and Norman Charles, who called themselves the Royal Kangaroos from Australia. It became pretty obvious early on that Boyd was messing with me, testing me. Occasionally, someone will do that to you — they'll put you in a hold and cinch down on you, go beyond just working, and see how far they can push you.

It's not really a smart thing to do to a guy with my background. I didn't really get all that mad; I knew he was just testing me. So I "tapped" him — which means I busted him in the face with a legitimate fist. I knocked him to the ground. He decided he didn't want to test me any more. I guess that means I passed!

That only happened to me that once. Generally, there's a pretty close camaraderie among wrestlers. They always refer to themselves and each other as the boys. You're all very dependent upon each other to earn your living. The guys who don't play fair don't last very long, with a few unfortunate exceptions.

None of this worried Terry as much as you might think, at least while it was just the two of us. She knew what the life of a wrestler was like before she married me, and she'd volunteered to be part of it. She knew I'd always find a way to come through. But in 1979 we had a new reason to start taking the risks and the drawbacks of a wrestler's life a good bit more seriously.

His name is Tyrel. Headstrong and independent to this day, Ty showed up about a month earlier than we were expecting him. I was in the delivery room with Terry the whole time on the night he arrived, and the minute the doctors placed him in my arms, he looked up at me and smiled. I'll never forget it. I named him after one of my favorite Western book characters, Tyrel Sackett from author Louis L'Amour.

Like a lot of preemies, Tyrel was a little on the small side at birth, but within a few months he grew to mammoth proportions.

Today, at age nineteen, he's six foot seven; he towers over most people, including his old man.

He's been a terrific kid, son, and young man. He's been through some things that most kids don't have to experience. When he was four, his sister Jade was born with seizures, and he had to witness the trauma that she went through. It was remarkable how he was able to deal with it all.

One time, Terry and I went to a Bob Dylan concert. Just before Dylan came on-stage, we got a call from my mom, who was up at the lake cabin watching Ty and Jade. Jade had just gone into a seizure. My mom was a retired nurse, but when she saw Jade having her seizure, she sought Tyrel for advice. And when they arrived at the hospital, Ty, at age six, told the doctors Jade's entire history, and recited, calmly and intelligently, the name of every medicine she was on. He absolutely blew the hospital staff away. Tyrel has had to look after his little sister probably more than a kid should have to, but he's risen to it in a way that's nothing short of admirable.

He's got Terry's slender build and stunning eyes, but Terry's always saying that Tyrel's a lot like me. He's got that Janos independent streak. Once upon a time, I had the same dream for him to go to college that my folks had for me. I tried to pound it into him, but I guess I didn't pound hard enough. Either that or no amount of pounding would have made a difference. He's following his own path. He's a born filmmaker. He's totally bitten by the film industry. Once I gave him a few hundred dollars to spend however he wanted, and he bought a device that allowed him to lay down film soundtracks. He'll eventually find his way out to Los Angeles and go to film school.

He's charting his own course, doing it his way, in the words of Frank Sinatra. I've never discouraged him. When I got into my film career, I brought him on set a few times. He was even in a movie with me, an independent sci-fi film I did in Canada called *Abraxas*. He played a bully. (That's the great thing about independent films; they'll hire your relatives.) I got out of the way and let the director work with him. Tyrel's built his own connections in the film industry. He's been out to see Joel Schumacher, the director. When it's time for him to go out there, he'll have no trouble at all making his way.

From about the time Tyrel was seven until just recently, he and I used to go "patrolling" on the Mississippi River. We'd get camouflaged up, lock and load, and get into our inflatable raft. Terry would drop us off at our insertion point, then pick us up at a prearranged extraction point downstream a few hours later.

Our patrolling ended up causing Terry more than a little bit of embarrassment. She was waiting for us at the pickup spot one morning when two police officers drove up. They said, "Ma'am, we just got a report of two terroristic-looking individuals going down the river, looking like they're up to no good. Have you seen them?"

Terry answered sheepishly, "Um, yes, actually, they're my son and husband. I'm waiting for them."

The two police officers turned to each other and said, "Ah, it's just Mr. Ventura again." I already had a reputation!

I'm pretty sure the incident that launched that reputation was the one that took place one night up in the woods where Terry and I used to live. We had a little house right near a log cabin that Terry's folks own now. Back then, that cabin was owned by the daughter of my father's best friend, who rented it out to a bunch of rowdy kids that summer. It was getting toward the end of the season, and the kids were getting ready to leave the next day, so they were having one last big blowout that night.

A bunch of Harley bikers were there, and they were out in the woods partying till all hours. That was fine, but at about three in the morning, they started getting really loud, and they woke me up. I had the kids by then, and I didn't want them being kept up by all the noise. Plus, I knew that when they were done partying, they were going to fire up the Harleys and roar out of there with a tremendous racket. Now I'm all for a good party, but there's got to be a limit to everything. And these kids were really starting to push the limit.

So I got out of bed and into my cammies, painted my face, put all my web gear on, pulled out my AR-15 assault weapon, and locked and loaded. As I was headed out the door, Terry woke up and came out, saw how I was dressed, and said, "My God, what are you doing?"

I said, "I'm going to put an end to the party."

I slipped out the door, took about twenty minutes to sneaky-crawl, SEAL style, up to their campsite — in fact, I looped around and came in on them from the opposite side. At one point, as I was lying there, one guy walked out from the campsite, stopped literally no more than four feet from me, urinated, and went back to the party, never having any idea I was there.

At the appropriate time, I walked into the center of the camp. Can you imagine? Most of the partyers are probably half out of it, smokin' pot and drinkin' beer, and all of a sudden this six-foot-four monster appears out of the woods, fully loaded with weapons, right in the middle of their camp.

I told them, very quietly, "Well, I'd have three confirmed kills on you guys right now, if I wanted them. But don't worry, I'm friendly forces."

I looked them all up and down, real slow. All I could see was row upon row of frightened, bleary eyeballs staring at me. "The party's too loud." I told them, "It's time for the party to end now. I'm going to disappear again, as quietly as I came. But there's a lot of Harley-Davidsons here. I want them all walked out to the road and started there, not here." And I narrowed my eyes at them and growled, "Don't make me come back." Then I turned and disappeared back into the woods.

They sat there for a while and didn't say a word. And lo and behold, every Harley got walked out to the road.

A couple of weeks later, I walked into the

local gas stop a half mile from the house, and two Brooklyn Park police came up to me. They said, "Hey Jesse! We heard you broke up a party along the river the other night — you did our job for us!"

"How did you know about that?" I asked.

They laughed, "My God, that story's spread all over town! We heard you used pretty good technique!"

"Well, they had me outnumbered about fourteen to one, so I had to let 'em know I was serious and that the advantage was mine."

So word was spread that occasionally I would do some strange things along the riverbank. Well, it was my riverbank. I was the captain of the river.

Patrolling was good training for Tyrel, too. Whenever we went out, we took it very seriously. We did everything by the books. When you go out on ops, there's no talking. So when Ty and I went out, it was in complete silence; all hand signals. It was good discipline.

I did that for a reason. I believe very strongly that guns are instruments of death. That's all they're used for; there's no purpose for them other than to kill. I think you have to understand that in order to respect them. I have no fear of my son handling weapons, because he has that respect. I remember the first time I let him shoot my M-16. He was just a young kid. I took him up to the lake, I set up a target range, and I let him shoot. He fired it three or four times, then he set the weapon down, walked away, and sat down. I asked him, "What's the matter?"

He said, "I kinda . . . just need to rest a little, Dad."

I told him, "See? It's not like the movies, is it? This is real."

And he understood. What you see in the movies, and what you pretend when you play cops and robbers and that sort of thing, is very different than what you're doing when you fire the real thing. You know that those projectiles you're firing could kill. That's what they're designed to do.

Ty's a well-rounded, good kid. He's also a gentle kid — he'll walk away from a fight; he's not like his old man. I admire him for it. It's a quality I wish I had more of in myself. I don't walk away from a confrontation.

There was recently a unique story on the editorial page of the Minneapolis *Star Tribune*: They compared me to a Klingon. There was even a little drawing of me, with the caption, "Governor Klingon." The guy who wrote the article explained that

Klingons are very honorable; they believe in things. And if you draw a line in the sand, they'll fight you to the death for what they believe in. When I read the story, I thought it was very accurate.

I have two great kids, in spite of the somewhat unusual upbringing they've had. Even though the odds in the wrestling business are stacked against the wrestler half a dozen different ways, I managed to make a fairly decent living at it. Terry and I swore that we wouldn't start a family until we could provide for one properly, and we were married for five years before we got to that point.

There were a number of times in my career, though, when wrestling went bad on me. There were dark patches in those years that were marked by backstabbing and betrayal. I once had a close friend you've probably heard of. His name was Hulk Hogan. Like me, he was a disciple of "Superstar" Billy Graham. Like me, he turned rebel on the twenty-six-region system and threw his lot in with Vince McMahon at the founding of the modern WWF. He was Vince's golden boy, the favored son. He was fed up with the unfair working conditions we wrestlers faced, just as I was. But it turned out that he had his own way of dealing with it, which led to the end of our friendship.

Wrestling, you see, is unlike other sports in that it's not a simple contest of athletic ability. There are a whole lot of other intangibles that go into it. Wrestlers are close with each other as a rule, but there's an element of competition in there, too, because we're all vying for that push from a promoter that can make or break your career.

All through your wrestling career, remember, you're an independent contractor. You're paying out an enormous amount in taxes. There's no pension, no health benefits. And the moment you're not making that draw, the promoters couldn't care less about you. You're a piece of meat. I knew guys that had worked hard for twenty years or more and still retired with nothing. Wrestling operated under some of the most unfair working conditions in the country. I don't know how they got away with it for so many years. The WWF was supposed to change things, but it hadn't turned out that way.

I had been rumbling quietly about forming a wrestler's union for a while. One day I had met up with Gene Upshaw, the union rep for the National Football League, in an elevator. Gene looked at me, and in that big deep voice of his said, "You boys in wrestling need to unionize!"

170

And I said, "You're right, Gene, we do!" Ever since then, I had been talking quietly among the boys. They were all for it. All we had to do was to wait for the right moment, which came pretty soon after that.

It was spring of 1987. We were scheduled for the WWF's Wrestlemania II in Los Angeles. All the publicity had gone out on it already. About two weeks before the event, I went into a dressing room full of wrestlers and said, "Boys, if there was ever a chance to organize, now is the time to do it. All of our faces are on the Wrestlemania publicity — the fans are expecting us. They couldn't back out of the deal now. Now's our chance."

But a couple of the wrestlers said, "We need Hulk Hogan. We can't do this without him."

"No, we don't," I explained. "Hogan's scheduled to wrestle King Kong Bundy, and Bundy has publicity out on him already. If Bundy backs us, Hogan has to wrestle him. If we all stick together and simply tell Vince we're refusing to wrestle unless we're allowed to unionize, what are they gonna be able to do? And if the other unions all back us up, who's gonna turn the lights on in the building?" Vince had invested millions in Wrestlemania II. We had him.

But nobody wanted to be the one to risk it. They were all behind me until I started drawing heat for it. Then I was alone. I came home a few nights later, and as soon as I walked in the door the phone rang. It was Vince McMahon. I knew something big was going down because he's not in the habit of calling his wrestlers at home for a chat.

"Ventura, what are you trying to pull? I heard you were trying to unionize wrestling."

I thought to myself, "Who told him?" But I'm not the type to back down from anything, so I said, "Yeah, I'm looking into it. Why wouldn't I? This is not to fight you, Vince. This is about me and all the other wrestlers who have to pay four or five thousand a year for health care. If we're in a union, we can buy it in bulk and save a lot of money." I went on to tell him all the reasons why unionizing would help us. But he argued and threatened, and we basically got nowhere. I told him, "Jeez, Vince. This is just like the movie *Norma Rae*."

For years and years, I wanted to know who had squealed on me. It was just me and the other wrestlers in the room that night, so it had to have been one of them. A few years later, I faced Vince McMahon in a court of law, and that's when the truth came out.

Fortunately for me, I soon had another option. I had just been signed to do the movie *Predator* and had appeared on the TV show *Hunter* before that. I was now eligible for my Screen Actors Guild card. I had my union. To this day, I keep my dues paid, because that's where I get my health and retirement benefits.

Once my SAG card had kicked in, I told Vince, "Don't worry. I'm not going to try to unionize anymore. I have my union card. If those guys are too gutless to do it, let them find their own way into a union."

Even after I left the WWF, Vince McMahon still found ways to exploit me. He was very big into marketing, and he had my voice and likeness on about ninety videotapes that he had for sale. I had asked him once why he was making all this money off of me, yet I wasn't seeing a dime of it. He'd said, "C'mon, Ventura. Nobody gets royalties off of videotape. Hulk Hogan doesn't even get royalties. Why would you?" And I believed him.

Later in my career, I developed a friendship with an ally who started smartening me up to this kind of thing. His name was Barry Bloom, and aside from being a die-hard wrestling fan, he was also a Hollywood talent agent. He liked to watch wrestling at night in his hotel room when he was on business trips, and he'd seen this big powerful blond guy with a feather boa and a commanding presence, and he was convinced that I was perfect for the movies.

Barry is a terrific guy. He's right at home with my particular brand of strangeness. He's game for just about everything. He's pretty good on a horse. He's even been out patrolling with me and Tyrel.

We took Barry out to the little island in the river we used to camp on. We got in there at night and made our camp and set up booby traps with flares, in case anybody came up on us at night. Ty had a little plastic gun; I had my AR-15, loaded. I never carry one that isn't. In the morning, we cleared up our camp, packed up our booby traps, and made it look like no one had been there.

When we were coming back up to the house, I told Barry to hide behind a hill. When Terry came out, I got a worried expression on my face and said, "Where's Barry? We left him an hour ago. He's not here?"

Terry was about to panic. "You left him down at the river all by himself? That guy from L.A.?" That's when Barry stepped out from behind the hill, in hysterics.

I was the first wrestler in history to ever

bring in an agent. From then on, Barry negotiated with the WWF for me, and he kept bringing up the subject of royalties. But each time he did, he was told that no one in the WWF gets royalties for videotapes — just as I had been told earlier, with only one exception. So I figured that if no one was getting royalties, what chance did I have? Barry also told me that I had a right to protect the use of my likeness. So I filed a federal trademark on "Jesse 'The Body' Ventura."

I actually took Vince McMahon's company to court over the royalty issue. I sued on what's called "quantum meruit" for the fair value of my contributions to his videos. As it turned out, I had been lied to for several years, because Hulk Hogan and others were getting royalties for their videotapes. And the court agreed with me that had I known the truth, I would not have agreed to perform unless I got royalties too.

We learned that Vince had made $25 million from the ninety videotapes I was on. When they applied a fair royalty rate to those tapes, it came out to about $800,000. And after interest was added in, I walked away from that lawsuit with about a million dollars. I made an enemy of Vince McMahon that day. Since I'd beaten him in court, he wasn't ever going to hire me again. It doesn't behoove promoters to have wrestlers who know what their rights are.

During the lawsuit, I took my lawyer, David Olsen, aside and asked him, "If the opportunity comes up . . . could you see if you can get McMahon to tell who it was that squealed on me about the union?"

So during Vince's deposition, David asked, "Mr. McMahon, has there ever been a union in wrestling?"

"No."

"Has anyone ever tried to form a union?"

"Yeah. As a matter of fact, I think Jesse Ventura spouted his mouth off about it."

"Were you in the room?"

"No, I wasn't."

"Well, then how did you know about it?"

Without any hesitation, Vince replied, "Hulk Hogan told me."

I didn't show any emotion at the time, but I almost fell over in my chair. Hulk Hogan had been a friend of mine, or so I thought, for six or eight years at that point. He was the last person I would have suspected. It was then I knew that he was a traitor. In my mind he was the ultimate stooge. It turned out that Vince was taking care of him very well, and I guess he didn't want to share any of that with the other wrestlers. It came out in court that in one Wrestlemania, for example, he got paid more than all the rest of us combined.

Now, I fully acknowledge that he's the biggest star wrestling's ever had, I don't want to take any of that from him. But for him to pretend to be friends with all of us while all the while going behind our backs and telling Vince everything we said, and to ultimately stop us from unionizing, which would have made life better in countless ways for all of us, is pretty sad. From that point on, I lost all respect for him.

And that's how it is to this day. Later in my career, I was working for Ted Turner's World Championship Wrestling (WCW); I was not small potatoes. But Hogan came into the organization, and within three months I was fired. That's the power he has in wrestling. He knew that I know the true Hulk Hogan, so he didn't want me around. Besides, he wanted my act. Just look at him. He's going for the same look I had fifteen years ago.

That was by no means all of it. Back in the eighties, when steroids were legal, wrestlers were eating them like candy. It was accepted. Then all of a sudden, when Ben Johnson got caught using them in the 1992 Olympics, they became the Scourge of Humanity.

I had been talking about them for years, saying, "Doesn't anybody else out there see what's going on?" Steroids came into wrestling with the advent of the bodybuilder physique popularized by "Superstar" Billy Graham, who suffers grave medical problems today from his past use. Not only do they shorten your life, but guys who took a lot of them were susceptible to what became known as " 'roid rage." They'd suddenly snap under the slightest pressure and would go into a frenzy.

There was a doctor I won't name who made his living providing steroids to wrestlers. Wrestlers went to see him and left with their hands full of pills, no questions asked. The promoters drove wrestlers so hard that their bodies never could have withstood the punishment they were taking without them. They became a necessary evil. I'll be the first one to tell you — I used them occasionally myself. I would take testosterone for thirty days, then I'd go off it for nine months. But I later found out they were destructive. I even did a poster for the FDA once, explaining that I once took them and warning kids not to use them.

But when steroids became such a great evil in the public's eye, Hogan went on Arsenio Hall's national TV show and told the world that he had never used steroids except under doctors' orders for an injury. His big mantra to the kids at that time was to take their vitamins, work out, and say their prayers. I used to laugh at him and say, "What kind of 'vitamins,' Hogan? Orals or injectables?" Many wrestlers in the United States knew he used them. And yet he had the gall, on Arsenio Hall, to call "Superstar" Billy Graham, who was a hero and the number-one inspiration to both of us, a drug abuser for using them.

I broke new ground in wrestling in a lot of different ways. That's why I can't work in the business today. I've been banned because I'm known as a rebel. They know I'll stand up for myself, and that I know what my rights are. I made a lot of headaches for them.

My wrestling career was marked by deceit, betrayal, and broken friendships. But the low points were balanced out with some phenomenal high points. The moment I look back on as the most memorable of my career was when I wrestled Bob Backlund in 1981 for the WWF world title in Madison Square Garden. The standard saying in wrestling was that the heels drew the crowds, and I drew 'em that night. I was scheduled to go into the ring with Backlund three times in a row. The place was sold out. That was the highlight of my career: selling out three times in the mecca of ring sports. I don't know how I could have topped that.

I'm sure my world tour against Hulk Hogan would have been another great high point, if it had happened. This was a few years before his betrayal and the end of our friendship, and when both of us were enjoying a huge amount of popularity. Hogan was the world champ at that point. We were scheduled to go "around the Horn" together, wrestling in a whole bunch of cities all around the globe. It would have been one of the biggest draws in wrestling history and a great moment for both of us. But as it turned out, whatever force was at work that night at SEAL Cadre when I went over that dam and lived to tell about it was working its influence on my life again. Fate had other plans for me.

CHAPTER 6

"THE MOUTH"

It happened that fast — the beginning of the end of my wrestling career. One day I was wrestling in Phoenix, two days later I was flat on my back in a San Diego hospital in intensive care, with doctors telling me not to move and calling Terry to tell her I could die at any minute.

That night in Phoenix, I had known I wasn't at my best. Through the whole match, I couldn't get enough air. I thought it was just because I was a Minnesotan, used to cold weather, and Arizona's hot fall air was messing with my metabolism.

But it hit me again the next night when I was wrestling in Oakland. I was running out of breath in the ring; I couldn't get enough air. I was getting through the matches, but it was becoming extremely hard to keep going.

At that time I was hanging with Big John Studd, and he and I were planning to go to a gym to work out. But I told him, "John, I'm gonna go to bed; I'm not feeling good."

The next morning, we were scheduled to fly to San Diego, my last match before the start of the big program with Hulk Hogan for the title. John and I were going to go to the gym again. That was the routine: You flew into the city in the morning, then checked into your hotel, worked out, and rested and ate until it was time for your match in the evening. That morning, we checked into a Travelodge and were going to go to Jack Lambert's gym. Again, I told John to go on without me, and I went to bed.

I woke up at about one in the afternoon, drenched in sweat. Whenever I took a deep breath, I'd get hit with such severe pain in my lungs that I couldn't stand it. I'd had pneumonia a few years earlier, and I thought I was getting it again, because it was the same kind of severe ache in my lower back and searing pain in my lungs. But even when I'd had full-blown pneumonia, I was in such good shape that when I breathed into one of those devices that test your lung capacity, I took it all the way to the top. So when I checked myself into Sharp Cabrillo Hospital that Saturday afternoon, I didn't think I had all that much to worry about. I told them who I was and that I thought I was having another bout of pneumonia.

The doctor did some preliminary tests on

me, then came back into the room with a grave expression on his face. He told me, "I want you to sit in that chair, and I don't want you to move — sit and do not move!"

This doctor was an ex-marine, and I had told him that I'd been a SEAL, so we had a special understanding between us. I looked him in the eye and said, "C'mon, Doc, give it to me. What's the deal here?"

He said, "I don't think you have pneumonia. I think you have pulmonary emboli."

"What's that?"

"Blood clots in your lungs."

"What!"

He shook his head, "I'm telling it to you straight. If one of the clots breaks loose and travels to your heart, you could have a heart attack. If one travels to your brain, you could have a stroke."

They called in another doctor to give me an angiogram. Ever had one? They're interesting. I had to be awake through the whole procedure. They cut me open at the groin and ran a tube up through my heart and out the heart valve, and they then shot dye into my lungs so they could see if I had clots. Both lungs were packed with them.

They immediately immobilized me, put me on intravenous heparin to dissolve the clots, and had me on a twenty-four-hour monitor screen in the nurses' station so they could keep an eye on me. They brought in one of Southern California's top lung specialists, Dr. Applestein. He called Terry and told her, "You'd better fly out. He could die at any moment."

I was in intensive care with Terry at my side for six days, until they determined that the heparin had dissolved all the clots.

I was supposed to have started wrestling Hogan by then. We had already sold out at the Los Angeles Sports Arena. I would have made a huge amount of money. But I had to cancel the tour because I was going to be on Coumadin, a blood thinner, for sixty days. Coumadin keeps the clots from forming, but it also makes you a bleeder. If I had been injured in the ring while I was on Coumadin, any bruises or cuts I received would have just kept on flowing until I died.

I never got my matches with Hogan. I guess I must have lost about a million dollars on that deal. It was a chance of a lifetime, gone. I was stuck at home, recuperating, face-to-face with the fact that even if I was able to get back in the ring after this, there would eventually come a day when I couldn't wrestle anymore. It's a traumatic moment for any professional athlete to face: What do you do when it's over? What happens when your body can't perform any-more? What do you put on your résumé? Where do you go from here?

Now, long before this, even before I real-ized to what depths I was getting shafted by wrestling's powers that be, I had already been making plans for the inevitable day when I had to move on. But what I had come up with on my own, before the blood clots took up residence in my lungs, would never have taken me where I went next.

I had already opened Ventura's Gym, a weight-lifting center in Minneapolis. I ran the place for five years while I continued to wrestle. It made me more powerful in my run-ins with Vince McMahon and his ilk because they knew I had it to fall back on if I ever got kicked out of wrestling.

In the end, though, it was steroids that drove me out of the gym business. Guys came in to work out and shot up steroids in the bathroom. I found used syringes in the trash cans. The last thing I needed was for a mother and child to come into my gym and see a bunch of guys shooting up. But I couldn't control it. I even put up a sign telling people not to bring gym bags into the bathrooms. It was like adult day care. Finally, I got fed up with the whole thing, closed the gym, and leased out the space to

Domino's Pizza. Looking back now, I'm glad the gym didn't work out, because however secure it might have been, it could only have taken me so far.

Out of bad comes good sometimes. I believe in fate; I believe things happen for a reason. I look back now on the closing of the gym and my battle with the pulmonary emboli as things that had to happen to clear the way for what came next. It was through that adversity that a whole new phase of my life opened up.

One afternoon when I was pretty close to being fully recuperated from the emboli, I got a call from Vince McMahon. (This was before I sued him, remember.) He said, "I have an idea. . . . There's never been a bad guy on the microphone. Somebody who will do color commentating and side with the villains. Do you think you could do it?"

I said, "Sure I can." And that's how I started making my transition from the mat to the microphone. Out of that adversity came my broadcasting career.

In retrospect, I can see it was the wake-up call I needed to start moving into the next phase of my life. It couldn't have come at a better time. A couple years before this, in 1983, Terry and I had welcomed the birth of our daughter, Jade. I now had the three of them to take care of. I hadn't realized it yet at that point, but wrestling had taken me about as far as it could, and I needed to go a lot further in life.

Tyrel had been born early; Jade came late. I was right there in the delivery room for her birth, just as I had been for Ty's. But we knew something wasn't right when, the moment after she was born, they took her away from us.

Jade was having seizures. The doctors who examined her claimed she had even been having them when she was still inside Terry. At first, nobody could figure out what was wrong with her. After they did a CAT scan on her, a doctor informed us that whole parts of her brain were missing. He told us she'd most likely go through life in a vegetative state and that it would probably be best if we institutionalized her. Well, there was no way in hell Terry and I were going to do that.

Can you imagine just having given birth and being told that? It's pretty hard to take. Thankfully, it turned out that the doctor was wrong. When someone has seizures, it can cause pockets of fluid to build up on the brain. On the CAT scan, the fluids obscure the view of whatever's behind them, which is why it looked like parts of Jade's brain were missing. Her brain was all there. Rest assured, this was one young lady who was not destined to be a vegetable.

But the seizures continued. We had to go home from the hospital without her. For sixty days, Jade was in intensive care. We went to the hospital to visit her every day and went home and cried each night. We handled it in our own ways, together and separately. We swore to get her the very best care we could, and we were determined she wasn't going to go through life as a phenobarbital junkie in an institution somewhere. No matter what happened, we were determined to make life as normal for her as possible. But there is no nightmare in the world like knowing that something is threatening your child's life and that you're powerless to do anything about it.

Meanwhile, the doctors were trying to figure out what exactly was wrong. They'd never encountered something like this before, so they were trying to figure it out by a process of elimination.

Finally, they brought in Dr. John McDonald from the Courage Center in Minneapolis. Dr. McDonald was a neurological specialist. He knew of one other case like Jade's: a child in Florida who had a form of epilepsy that manifested in seizures like

Jade's. He sent for the records of the case and found out that the problem was an inability to metabolize vitamin B6, which is important for the central nervous system. Dr. McDonald put Jade on massive doses of B6, and, sure enough, her seizures stopped.

We brought her home, and she was seizure free and doing great until she reached age two. That's when the government expects you to have your child inoculated with the DPT vaccine against diphtheria, pertussis, and tetanus. They now know that the vaccine has a bad effect on kids who are susceptible to seizures, but back then, it was only a theory, so they insisted that every kid go through with it, in spite of the accumulating evidence. So Jade got her DPT shot.

I was out of town on a wrestling tour that day. In the middle of the night, in my hotel room, I suddenly woke up. A wave of apprehension broke over me, and I went from a dead sleep to wide-awake. Five minutes later, the phone rang. I picked it up and said, "What's wrong?"

Terry said that, after two years free, Jade had gone into heavy seizures and that they were on their way to the hospital. So tell me that there's not some kind of telepathic connection between people who are very close.

Jade was OK that time, but we refused to

let anybody give her more DPT vaccine shots. It was the government's fault she had to go through that, but there's no way you can sue over it. People have tried. Even though the government knows there are kids who are susceptible to seizures from the shots, they have plausible denial, since there are usually so many other things wrong with those kids. In fact, one of my top security officers has a child similar to Jade. He sued — spending twelve thousand dollars of his own money — and still couldn't win.

To this day, Jade has never gotten any more of those immunity shots. Whenever some government official rumbles about Jade needing to have them to go to school, we say, "OK, but put it in writing that you're ordering her to do this in spite of her medical condition, so we can sue you if she goes into seizures." None of them will do it.

Jade still has to take daily doses of vitamin B6. She's a special-ed kid, and Terry and I have fought to keep her in the mainstream with her classmates. She's the reason I'm a big advocate of mainstreaming special-ed kids — I've seen the miracle it's worked on Jade.

She's doing great. She's a remarkable young lady. She plays basketball, and she's an accomplished horsewoman — she's won trophies and ribbons. And she has an extraordinary way with animals, which a lot of special-ed kids seem to have. Every animal on the planet is her friend. Jade once brought a baby snapping turtle home from the lake. That turtle, whom she named Ed, got to recognize her voice and came when she called him. She fed him little shrimps from the end of a pair of tweezers. Ed's been released back to the wild now, but his successor, Speedy, is quickly figuring out that the sound of Jade's voice means it's time to eat.

Jade is a wonderful, sweet, well-mannered kid with a heart of gold. And she's tough as nails, because she had to fight for her life from the day she was born. She has her own unique take on the story of her birth. Do you know what she says about the whole mix-up that happened at her birth, when the doctors thought she was going to be a vegetable? She says, "I tricked 'em."

Jade was the reason I "defected" to the WWF and joined up with Vince McMahon in the first place. Her medical bills were severe, and my health plan covered only a portion of them. We were deeply in debt. Remember, there was no union, no great medical policy. I felt I had to set my ego aside. My daughter's life was more important than Jesse "The Body" and his ego. I believe in paying my debts, and I don't go looking to welfare to do it. I take responsibility for my own actions, and I don't expect the government to come and bail me out. I knew what I had to do for my daughter.

I had been working for Verne Gagne in the Minnesota territory until recently. He was a yeller and a screamer, and he didn't treat people right. I had quit working for him, and I didn't like the idea of having to ask him to hire me back, but the money had to come from somewhere so I could pay for Jade's treatment. I wasn't wrestling at all at the time because I was busy running my gym. I told Verne my daughter was in intensive care and asked him if I could come back. He saw this as an opportunity to stick it to me and said, "I can't use ya." Now, I was a Main Eventer, I was a big draw at the time, so I knew this was bullshit.

So I called Vince McMahon out east at the WWF. Vince said, "Look, Jesse, don't worry about it. You're over strong out here. I'll tell you what: I'll only book you on the weekends — Friday, Saturday, and Sunday — so you can be home with your daughter during the week."

Well, after that, Verne called — he'd suddenly gotten a whiff of money — and said, "Look, Jesse, I just lost a guy here. Why don't you come back and take his place." So I called Vince and told him I had full-time work again.

Vince said, "Well, Jesse. Maybe this is working out for the best. Go back and work for Verne for now. But I'll tell you what. In a few months, I'm gonna call you. And when I do, I want you to come and work for me, full-time. Something big is gonna happen, and when it does, I want you working with me."

"Vince, if I do that, I won't just be burning my bridge with Verne, I'll be exploding it."

Vince said, "The choice is yours."

Now in spite of what Verne had done to me, I still had to think long and hard about cutting my ties with him. I'm a very loyal person. But later, Verne made the decision for me.

I went back to wrestling for Verne. I was in a tag match with Masa Saito from Japan, who I call "Mr. Torture," because if anybody gets out of line, Saito will beat the shit out of them. When he and I decided to go back into the steel-cage tag match together, the house gross went up by about $7,000. But somehow, Saito and I got $100 less. The house was bigger, we were the Main Event — the whole reason the house was bringing in more money — yet we were getting less. Now how did that happen? Later on, we found out that Verne and his son had just gone on a big skiing trip to Aspen and somebody had to pay for it!

So a few months later, when Vince called, I went. Verne had butchered my allegiance to him by trying to yank my chain when I was in need and then added insult to injury by taking my money for his own personal pleasure. So I went with Vince and got into the WWF express elevator just as it was about to rocket its way up to international fame. Soon after that, Verne, and other regional promoters like him, went out of business.

Back in the days when wrestling was a twenty-six-territory sport, there was an unwritten rule that nobody crossed into anybody else's territory. Each of the promoters had his own little piece of America, and they all belonged to the NWA, the National Wrestling Alliance, which met yearly to discuss how to handle us wrestlers and how to keep us in our place.

Well, when Vince McMahon came along, he didn't owe any allegiance to the old guard. He was taking over from his father, Vince Senior, who had run the World Wrestling Federation in the Northeast, and who was dying of cancer. This was right at the time that cable television was coming in. Vince bought heavily into cable TV, and then started taking one or two of the top talent from each territory. He came to Minnesota and stole the announcer Gene Oakerlund, Hulk Hogan, and me from Gagne. He offered us a better deal and a chance to go national.

In essence, we were burning our bridges. All of the other promoters saw going with Vince as a betrayal, and if Vince failed, we had no place to go back to. Vince even got death threats. We all got notices saying, "What are you trying to pull, you sons of bitches? What are you trying to do to the wrestling business? You'll never wrestle again!" But I was so disenchanted with the wrestling business by then that I thought, "Screw it. I'm gonna take a chance."

But I hadn't done anything illegal. It was capitalism. It was just as if I'd been a ketchup maker and left Heinz to go make ketchup for Hunt's. The public just chooses which ketchup they want to buy. That's how free enterprise works. That's capitalism.

By joining the WWF, which was nationwide, I was getting in on the ground floor of something totally new, and I realized that if it worked, I'd be a bigger name than I could ever be regionally. And it was true. If I hadn't done that, Barry Bloom would never have seen me on cable TV in his hotel room.

Amusingly enough, years later when I sued Vince McMahon, Verne Gagne came in to testify against him on my behalf! He was one of my strongest witnesses. He explained, "I hate Vince McMahon even more than I hate Jesse Ventura!"

I had been on board with the WWF for a couple of years by the time I had the pulmonary embolism, and I launched my commentating career as soon as I was fully recovered. Vince flew me out to Toronto and made me an announcer with Gorilla Monsoon. Vince had two teams of announcers: The "A" team was himself and Bruno Samartino, who worked the best shows, and the "B" team was me and Gorilla.

I was coming over powerfully on the microphone. The TV audience loved to hear me talk about how much "highly developed skill" it took to pull someone's hair and hide it from the referee. I always covered for the bad guys. When the bad guys lost, I gave them great excuses. The people loved it! They'd say, "Yeah! Goddamn, he's right!"

I started building more and more momentum, becoming more powerful because

I was so good on the mike. Vince soon replaced Bruno with me. It was at that point that NBC came in and had me and Vince do Saturday Night's Main Event. Our producer, Dick Ebersol, named me "One-take Jesse." When they'd set up the cameras to film the promos, I'd nail them all in one take and go back to my trailer.

I broke new ground. I was the only person to get on the mike and announce, then get in the ring and wrestle, and then come back to the mike afterward. I'd say, "You don't see Howard Cosell doin' this, do ya? I'm the only announcer in the world who can back up what he says by getting in the ring and provin' it!"

I quickly became even more popular behind the microphone than I was on the mat, but I was no less outrageous. They called me, facetiously, wrestling's only "unbiased" announcer. I had a wardrobe to match my attitude. My commentating bits came to be known as the Jesse "The Body" Fashion Show because Vince put me in a different far-out costume each night. I wore tie-dyed tuxes, pink satin smoking jackets, feathers, earrings, peace signs, wild sunglasses — never the same outfit twice.

In fact, one night, when I was wearing a tie-dyed tux, a fan came up, shook my hand,

and asked in a deep Austrian accent, "Nice suit, where did you get it?" That was my first encounter with Mr. S., but it was by no means my last.

The NBC gig spawned a whole wave of others: I hosted Wrestlemania, I did color commentary for the Minnesota Vikings, I became the commentator for the Tampa Bay Buccaneers — fans came up and told me, "We love having you in the booth because you're like one of us. It's like having a fan in the booth."

I also appeared as the host of Get a Grip Night on the Movie Channel. The show featured wrestling flicks, and it was my job to introduce the film and comment on it during breaks. I hosted the show from a library set — very Alastair Cooke — tall shelves, shaded reading lamps, stacks of weighty leather-bound tomes piled all around, and in a stately wing-backed leather chair, this big wild-haired guy in tie-dye and feathers, reading Shakespeare. I'd look up at the camera and announce in a snooty tone, "Good evening. Welcome to Get a Grip Night on the Movie Channel, the only movie network not for geeks." At the end of the segment, I'd say something like, "That's all for now. It's time for me to . . . hit the books" — BAM!

I was the greatest announcer wrestling's

ever had, but I ended up getting banned from both leagues. I'm too independent; I don't kiss their asses. McMahon wouldn't work with me because I beat him in the lawsuit, so that rules out the WWF. Hogan wouldn't work with me because he knows I know what kind of man he really is. So that left me out of the WCW. It's their loss. I'm not hurting from it. And now that I'm in politics, our relationship has started to improve a little.

It's all politics. In some ways, wrestling politics aren't all that different from the brand of politics I'm dealing with now. Only now, I'm smarter and wiser than I was then. Toughing it out in the ring against hails of insults and dealing with all the backstabbing and betrayal and infighting — what better training is there for public office?

The commentating was a terrific boost all on its own, but the best thing about it was where it led me. A phone call woke me up early one morning when I was staying in a hotel in Saint Louis. It was one of the people at Titan Sports, the WWF's parent company in Connecticut. He was full of excitement: "Jesse! There's a Hollywood agent that has a movie role he thinks you'd be interested in. You wanna talk to him?"

I said, "Sure."

That's how I met Barry Bloom. He told me he thought I had a great presence on camera, and he just had a gut instinct that I'd be great in the movies. This was at a time when the whole world was going "Hulk this, Hulk that." And Barry was saying, "Yeah, Hulk's good, but have you seen this Jesse Ventura? He has more talent."

Barry and I got to talking back and forth, developing a rapport. His boss at the time, Mary Ellen White, kept asking, "Why are you spending all this time talking to that wrestler? He's never made us any money."

Barry replied, "He will."

So I told Vince to book me in California whenever he could. He said, "Oh, you like that sun out there, huh?"

I just grinned and said, "Yeah. I like the sun."

Barry got me on an episode of *Hunter*. We did it all aboveboard, through Vince and everything. But whereas Barry only took 10 percent of what I made, Vince took half! When I finally got my check, I called Barry and said, "Well, Barry, I got my seven hundred and fifty dollars for doing *Hunter*. What's the deal?" Barry was outraged. He told me I was getting shafted. So I said, "Screw Vince. I'm dealin' directly with you from now on."

The next time I came to L.A., Barry met me at the plane and shepherded me to his car, "You have a two o'clock appointment today with a lady named Jackie Burch. She's casting the next Schwarzenegger film."

Barry parked outside an office building on the Twentieth Century–Fox lot, and I went inside. That's how it's done — your agent never goes inside with you. I walked in, and this little lady walked up to me. I said, "Hello, I'm Jesse Ventura."

She said "Hi, I'm Jackie Burch." She couldn't take her eyes off me. She looked me up and down twice. Then she smiled and said, "Let's go meet the executive producers." She hadn't even given me a reading yet!

She walked me across the lot and into a huge, plush office where Joel Silver, John Davis, and Larry Gordon, the producers, sat waiting to meet me. Jackie introduced me to them and said, "I think we have our Sergeant Blain."

Jackie took me back to her office and handed me the script, which at the time was also called *Hunter*. The Sergeant Blain character was a six-foot-four, 250-pound professional killer. Perfect, though at the time I looked anything but military. I had bleached blond hair to my shoulders, three earrings in each ear, sunglasses, and a long goatee. I looked like a madman. But Jackie saw past all that. Sergeant Blain was me.

The line I read for her was one where Blain has just offered the other guys chewing tobacco, and they've turned him down: "Buncha slack-jawed faggots around here. This stuff'll put hair on yer hog leg. Make you a god-damned sexual ty-rannosaurus. Just like me." Even there I fit the role, because I chewed tobacco at the time. I could chew and spit — *pwttt!* — and make it look like I'd been doing it all my life.

Jackie said, "Here, take the whole script; read it."

Half an hour later, they called Barry with an offer.

Well, now I had a problem. I still worked for Vince McMahon. I flew back to Minneapolis, and I tried to call him. I kept getting the same runaround: "Vince is in a meeting; he's busy."

I said, "Look, it's extremely important. I only need Vince for five minutes — five minutes!"

They kept saying, "OK, we'll tell him."

Barry called and said, "Look, Jesse, the film company needs to know if you're taking the role, or else they're gonna look for someone else."

I told him, "OK, I'll try calling Vince again."

When I called Vince's line again, I got George Scott, Vince's booker. George said, "Jesse. Look. You can't get through to Vince."

"Why not?"

"Well, if you won't tell anyone else I told you, do you want to know what he said? He said that he doesn't have time for Jesse Ventura's personal problems."

I said, "That's cool. I'll tell you what, George. Don't hurry. Don't hurry. When he has time, if there's a break in the day, simply tell Vince that I've been cast in the next Arnold Schwarzenegger film and that I'm accepting. And I'll get back to him in due time. Thanks, George." Click.

I called Barry and told him I was accepting the role. Five minutes later, the phone rang. Guess who it was?

Vince sounded a mite pissed: "Well, Jesse, what's going on here?"

I said, "Vince, I've been offered a role in the next Arnold Schwarzenegger movie, and since I couldn't get through to you to let you know, I accepted."

"Who's the agent?"

"It's Barry Bloom."

Vince roared, "You tell Barry Bloom he's

fired! He doesn't do anything without clearing something like that through me!"

I said, "Vince, Barry don't work for you. He works for me."

"Well, you can't go do this. I need you for wrestling right now."

"Vince, wrestling will always be there. I'll never get another opportunity like this. I'm goin' to do this film. Tough luck."

So I quit. I did the commentating job on Wrestlemania II that I'd already agreed to do, then I left the very next day for Mexico to start shooting. While we were down there, the title of the film was changed to *Predator*. It was by far the best film of my career. People say I stole the film from Arnold. Fox even made a T-shirt with my famous line, "I ain't got time to bleed." Taking that role was one of the best decisions I've made in my life.

Even once I was down there, Vince was still trying to regain the control he'd lost. He sent his top *WWF Magazine* photographer, Steve Taylor, down to do a story about the shoot. Steve got a call from Vince and relayed a message to me: "Jesse, Vince wants you to call him immediately."

I said, "You tell Vince McMahon Jesse Ventura doesn't exist down here. Sergeant Blain is down here. I have nothing to do with wrestling here; I'm doin' a movie. You tell Vince he'll have to wait till I get back to the States."

The night before I flew to Mexico, I met up with Barry. It was a Sunday night. Late that evening, Barry suddenly said, "You've got your Declaration of Citizenship and everything, right?"

Jeez — I didn't even know I had to have one! We were running all around town like chickens with our heads cut off, trying to find a place open that could process a Declaration of Citizenship for me. We even went to the Beverly Hills police department. Nothing. Nada.

I put my head in my hands. "Are we fucked? Did I just torpedo my own film career before it even got started?"

Finally in the wee hours, we found a Declaration of Citizenship Form that we were told would do the trick. We came crawling into the airport the next morning, bleary eyed, and the guy who checked us in said, "Hey — this is filled out wrong. Here — have another one." He had a whole stack of blank forms right there at the airport!

Barry and I looked at each other, "God, are we a couple of idiots!"

Here's a little bit of cocktail-party trivia: before we flew down to Mexico, we met a guy who had been hired to work inside the Predator suit, an ambitious young kid who was trying to work his way into the business. Something about him impressed me. I told Barry, "Watch out for this guy. He's goin' places." Unfortunately, it turned out that Mexico wasn't one of those places, at least not on this shoot, since he later got fired from the film. But he eventually proved me right. His name? Jean-Claude Van Damme.

The guy who took over the suit work from Van Damme was Kevin Peter Hall, an absolutely terrific guy, a glow of light. He always had a smile on his face. He did extremely well for himself considering he was seven foot two — how many roles are there for somebody that tall? It saddened me a lot to learn that he died of AIDS. Hollywood lost someone special when it lost Kevin.

Hollywood is Hollywood, but when you get way, way out of town on location like we did, the cast and crew become a family. It's you guys against the world. Everyone becomes close-knit. I think the film turns out better because everyone's so focused. When you shoot in L.A., everyone goes home every night. On location, you live the project until it's done.

I got to be especially good friends with the stunt guys. They liked me because I wasn't afraid to get down and dirty with them. I did my own rappelling in *Predator*. They didn't want me to, but I've got to defy death occasionally, just for my own peace of mind. Sometimes, you need to defy death so that you can appreciate life more.

I admired the stuff the stunt guys did. I especially liked to watch the full-body burns, where they'd be entirely engulfed in flames. They asked me if I wanted to do that, and I asked, "How much does it pay?" They told me. I said, "Move the decimal point over a couple of times, then we'll talk."

The stunt guys and I had a mutual respect for each other, but the higher-ups, the above-the-line guys, took a little more convincing. I was a newcomer — I can understand why they didn't have a lot of confidence in my acting ability. But for a while there, they weren't even going to give me a chance to prove to them that I could do it.

One day while we were in Mexico, I was handed a bunch of new changes to the script. These new changes took some of the best lines away from my character and gave them to somebody else's. I wasn't going to let them do that. I went over to Joel Silver's trailer and asked to see him. They pulled the old Vince McMahon line, "He's in a meeting." Well, you can only hear "He's in a meeting" so many times. So I kicked open the door to his trailer and said, very calmly, "We gotta talk." Joel gave me back my lines.

It was during those weeks on location that Arnold Schwarzenegger and I got to be good friends. Arnold is terrific. He's a close friend to this day; he even flew into town for my inauguration. He's one of the most focused men I've ever met in my life. He's self-made; I respect him for that. He's achieved things that no one thought were possible. Arnold and I are parallel in a lot of ways. We don't believe in the word *can't*. Whenever somebody says we can't do something, we take that as a challenge. We become that much more focused. People told Arnold he couldn't become a movie star. They told him he'd have to change his name and lose his accent. Well, he's Arnold Schwarzenegger, and he's never lost the accent — and he's about as big a star as you'll ever find. He said the first agent he ever approached turned him down. Can you imagine how that guy's kicking himself today? He could have had 10 percent of that!

Arnold and I have the same love of simple pleasures. While we were shooting *Predator*, Arnold got me into stogies — a habit I enjoy to this day. It's very relaxing after a long day to put your feet up and disappear into a sweet-smelling cloud of smoke.

He's a generous guy. When he got down there, he had all of his gym equipment put into a room, and he gave a key to me and anyone else who wanted one and said, "Work out whenever you want to."

We got up in the mornings and worked out from five to six, because if we didn't Arnold would be on our cases all day: "Jesse, you didn't work out this morning. What's the matter with you?" He's a big teaser, but the nice thing is that he can take it just as well as he can dish it out.

So I started getting up at about quarter to five and getting into the gym before Arnold and his friend Sven (his bodyguard and double) came in. I would grab the mineral water and soak myself with it, so I would look like I was drenched in sweat. I would only be doing my first set when Sven and Arnold walked in, but Arnold didn't know that! He'd walk in and say, "Sven! Look at this! Who knows how long Jesse's been training! We must get up earlier. We can't let Jesse outtrain me!" So it ended up that we were both getting up earlier and earlier, until we were getting up at four in the morning!

I like to joke that I "coached" Arnold through his wedding to Maria Shriver.

While we were shooting, he was scheduled to leave the set for a few days to go get married. Before he left, I teased him that he'd have to remember to speak from the diaphragm and say clearly, "I do! I DO!" He'd be in front of the cameras ready to do a take, and I'd be off in a corner somewhere. Just as they were about to roll, I'd give him an "I DO!" and he'd break up. Then the director would get mad, and I'd have to keep quiet.

You had to mess with each other and have some fun to break up the monotony. On Sundays we never worked. They set up a big screen and a VCR, and we all sent home for our favorite movies. I had my copy of *True Grit* sent out — that great John Wayne classic that's one of my all-time favorites. Jim Tyson, who did wardrobe, and Carl Weathers were sitting near me, and while the movie was going Tyson and I kept doing the dialogue before it happened in the film.

Finally, Carl had had it: "I can't take this. I don't need to hear the movie twice!" He got up and moved to the other side of the room so he didn't have to hear me and Tyson! You tend to get a little crazy down there, so things like that amuse you. I went for ten weeks without seeing a TV, and I found out it was a blessing. We had to start using our minds again to entertain ourselves. I think we've become too dependent on that box to entertain us.

That isolation was good for my focus, and one of the things I focused on was learning as much as I could from Arnold. He's a phenomenal businessman. You can't help but admire the wealth he's attained. A few years later, I heard he'd turned down seventeen million dollars to do *Predator 2*. He said the timing wasn't right. He doesn't do things just for money. I said, "Arnold, how do you turn down seventeen million? I'd do it for half!"

Arnold teaches you by talking to you, which is why you always have to stay awake when you're around him. I was pretty naive about the ways of Hollywood back then. One day on set, Arnold told me, "Jesse, always remember, never read a script until the money's right."

"Well, Arnold, that's easy for you to say. You've got ten or twelve of them on your desk; you can pick and choose. I'm not afforded that kind of luxury."

"But Jesse, if you read the script before you've negotiated the money, then if you like the script you have a biased opinion, and you'll do it for less. And if you can't get the money right, you've wasted your time reading the script."

Then he stopped and looked me in the eye and said, "Jesse, in our business, we don't have time to waste."

Later, when he had asked me to do *The Running Man*, the negotiations got stuck. It was my second film, so I wanted a lot more money. I had my heart set on one figure, but the film company was thinking of another figure entirely. I was starting to be afraid I'd lose the role because I'd asked for too much money.

But one day I got a call from Arnold. First thing off the bat, he said, "Jesse. I thought you were going to do *The Running Man* with me."

I said, "Arnold, I'd love to do *The Running Man* with you. I want to do *The Running Man* with you. But Arnold . . . I can't read the script until the money's right!"

He burst out laughing. "Jesse, trust me. The script is fantastic. Just get the money right."

Amazingly, that afternoon, the film company called me back and said they'd meet my price. Now, I don't know this for a fact, but the rumor I'd heard was that Arnold had asked them, "What is he asking for?" They told him. And Arnold said, "Pay him."

Arnold and I are close today. Our families exchange Christmas presents each year. I was deeply honored when Arnold flew into town for my inauguration. He was right in the middle of shooting a film, too. But I guess when you get to his level of success, you have your own plane and can say, "I'm not working today. I'm going to Minnesota."

He presented me with a beautiful gift that now sits on my desk: two huge bronze eagles from the National Historical Society. I'm sure they're very expensive; they're extremely heavy. There's a plaque on the back that reads, "Jesse, you are a true leader. Your friend, Arnold."

And to show you what a shrewd businessman he is, do you know what he did while he was in town for the inauguration? He went down to his restaurant, Planet Hollywood, in the Mall of America, and he met with his staff of chefs and came up with a new menu item: the Jesse "The Mind" Melt Sandwich! It's delicious — a big slab of cheese-covered beef with a bit of a spark to it. But the clever part is that by launching the new menu item, he turned the visit into a business trip! He can write the whole thing off!

While I was waiting for the *Running Man* negotiations to sort themselves out, I called Vince and told him, "We have a problem now. Barry Bloom represents me in all my film work, in everything I do except for wrestling. Now, Vince, convince me why he shouldn't represent me in wrestling, too."

"Well, uh, we don't have agents in wrestling."

"Then you don't have me."

At that point, he'd lost me for ten weeks and seen how badly he needed me. I was a hot commodity, and launching a film career had only made me hotter. So he finally swallowed his pride and called Barry Bloom. Today, it's standard for a wrestler to have an agent. And Barry Bloom has become the mega-agent for wrestlers.

Before I brought in Barry, the standard was that if a wrestler wanted to have an agent, he'd get fired. But my popularity gave me leverage. I remember one time I said to Vince, "That's the secret to becoming a mega-star, isn't it? To go out and become famous at something else, and then come back."

Vince smiled at me and said, "You're learning, aren't you?"

I had that whole summer after *Predator* off. I was finally able to make a lifelong dream come true: I bought a Porsche. I got it off one of the stuntmen on the *Predator* crew for around thirteen thousand. I decided to drive it back to Minnesota myself, although I had a tough time convincing Terry to come with. She was so uncomfortable in that little thing, she could barely move. All the way home she kept threatening to bail out and take the next plane home.

That summer, I also decided to venture into rock 'n' roll. I put together my own band, Soldiers of Fortune. It was a great boost to my acting and commentating careers, because it gave me confidence in my voice. A lot of people, even Arnold, have said I have a great voice, but I'd never believed it. But I figured, if I could make it in rock 'n' roll, it must be true.

I was the lead singer, and I played harmonica. Terry was in it, too — she was one of the backup singers. I had a great solo in one original number called "The Soldier of Fortune Blues," a real heavy, bluesy tune that we'd play in the middle of the set to slow everything down.

I'd never played harmonica before, and at first I was so bad that Terry went behind my back to Mark Orion, the music arranger, and pleaded with him, "Is there any way we can get Jesse to stop playing harmonica?"

Mark replied, "Oh, no, we can't do that to Jesse. That's his thing!"

It was so awful, they decided to call what I was doing a new form of music, "new-wave harp." Finally I figured out that if you buy a harmonica tuned in the key of the song, you sound pretty good no matter what notes you blow. That's a little-known secret from the music business.

We cut a demo under the nonexistent record label Jade Records. We did some covers of great rock oldies — "Sympathy for the Devil," "Eve of Destruction" — and a couple of original pieces. During the concerts, when we got to the part of "Sympathy for the Devil" that goes, "to end this tale, just call me Lucifer, for I'm in need of some restraint," I'd hit the word "LUCIFERRR!!!" and two big explosions were supposed to go off. But the kid who was supposed to be doing them tended to daydream, and he missed his cue a lot. When you're getting very cheap help, it's hard to get someone overly professional. But we did all right. We even got "Eve of Destruction" onto a *Hitmakers* CD — we're sandwiched between Paul McCartney and Mötley Crüe.

It was great; I'd like to do it again. You never get too old for rock 'n' roll. I learned from that experience that it's not your voice, it's the soul you put into it. Case in point: Bob Dylan — he's one of the greatest artists of all time, and it's not because of the quality of his singing voice (excuse me, Bob). I really don't know whether or not we sucked, but we had a lot of fun.

Finally, at the end of that summer, negotiations sorted themselves out, and I got to do *The Running Man* with Arnold. That was a blast, too, but I had even more fun on the press junket Fox sent me on when *Predator* was about to come out. It was Arnold's idea — he knew I was a good talker and could sell the film well. For somebody who comes from working-class Minneapolis, it was a trip into the Twilight Zone. They don't pay you for a press junket, but they treat you like a star. We flew all over the country in Fox's corporate jet. Limos picked us up. I left with $235 in my billfold and didn't use a penny of it in the three weeks I was gone. The cheapest hotel room they put me up in was about $800 a night.

I wanted Terry to get in on this experience, so I mentioned to the Fox people that I wanted to bring her along at my own expense — I asked if I could use my frequent-flier miles to let her catch up with us in New York. "You *want* your wife along with you?" When I insisted that I did, somebody got on the phone and said, "Get a first-class ticket to fly Mrs. Ventura out to New York. And have a car to pick her up." Sure enough, she was there waiting for us when we got to New York. And Fox picked up the tab.

Arnold recommended that we stay at the Lowell Hotel. "I think you'll like it, Jesse. It's Maria's favorite." It's a quaint old place with only three suites per floor, with antiques and shelves full of leatherbound books everywhere. A lot of stars stay there because it's peaceful and secluded. It was a treat.

We were scheduled to appear with Arnold in Coconut Grove, that ritzy section of Miami, but he got called away for something else. So it was just me inside the limo, being met by the hotel manager and owner, being escorted to my suite (you know you've got a nice room when they have to open two doors), which had a baby grand piano and a four-person Jacuzzi in the bedroom. It brings out the devil in you, having that kind of wealth lavished on you. I relaxed back in my hot bubble bath at the end of the day and thought, "I wonder what the poor people are doing today." Isn't that awful?

It was Arnold's influence on me that put an end to my work with Vince McMahon. When I finally came back to work with Vince again, he found out that I was negotiating a deal to do a video game. Vince had video games of his own on the market, and he didn't want me out there competing. So he told me point-blank, "You do this video game and you can't work for me."

Now one thing you've probably guessed about me is that I can't be bluffed. It's the Klingon in me; it's an insult to my honor. So I said, "Vince, if you really don't want me to do the video game, buy me out of it." He refused. So I did the video game. But that wasn't the last time Vince ever asked me to work for him again — just the last time I accepted.

After *Predator,* my film career took off. I did *The Running Man* with Arnold, then I did *Demolition Man, Major League 2,* a couple of indies called *Thunder Ground* and *Abraxas,* even an episode of *The X-Files.* I did outrageous Miller Lite and Campbell's Chunky Soup commercials. In 1990, I almost had my own TV series, but it wasn't in the cards.

It would have been an outstanding family-style TV show, if the network hadn't killed it. It was called *Tag Team.* The concept for the show came from a six-year-old kid, the son of a Hollywood writer. He and his dad were watching wrestling one night, and the kid said, "Gosh, Dad, you know what would be a neat story? Two wrestlers who become cops." Boom. That's how the whole thing started.

It was the story of two pro wrestlers who got banned from wrestling by a corrupt promoter and went on to become cops. Roddy Piper and I had the leads. My character was an ex–Navy SEAL — can't imagine where that idea came from! We had the entire writing team from *Magnum, P.I.*; they had written nine episodes. It was fun, light-hearted comedy, the kind where right always prevails over wrong.

The show's big hook was that as cops, we never used guns against our suspects; we always brought 'em in with nothing but our bodies, our wrestling technique, and our street smarts. We did all our own stunts, so they didn't have to do all those hard cuts that you see when a stunt man is used.

We made a pilot, which got snapped right up. It was great. Barry Bloom's agency partner Michael Braverman came down to watch the filming of the pilot. Michael's a terrific guy, but I did have to teach him a thing or two about wrestling. Once when Mike and I were talking about pro wrestling, he committed the cardinal sin. He used the *f* word. He said, "Everybody knows that's stuff's all fake. Isn't it?" I just narrowed my eyes at him a little. No need to say anything right then — actions speak louder than words.

So when Michael came to the set of *Tag Team*, I "helped" him (with Barry's help) see my side of it. We had a ring set up there, and I said, "Hey, Mike. Ever wonder what the inside of a pro wrestling ring feels like?"

He looked at me, puzzled. "Well, no, not really."

"Really? You've never been curious?"

Michael slipped a hand under the bottom rope and poked the mat with his finger. "Nice. Soft."

"Yeah, but haven't you ever wondered what it feels like to be in the ring? C'mon. Give it a try."

So Michael climbed into the ring with me. He bounced up and down on the mat a few times. "Nice ring."

That's when I grabbed him. I cartwheeled him head over heels and bounced him up and down a few times, letting his head stop just an inch or two from the mat each time. All the extras were screaming, "Kill the suit! Kill the suit!" They didn't know who he was. I wasn't going to do anything to him, I just wanted to let him know what I could do! He was clinging to me like a fly to flypaper. Then I flipped him right side up again and set him back on his feet. I said, "Still think wrestling's fake?" The discussion was over.

Tag Team never made it to the airwaves as a regular series, because the network decided it didn't fit their programming. They pulled the plug on it the night before we were scheduled to start shooting more episodes. We tried to get the rights to it — we were going to take it to Fox — but Disney wouldn't let it go, probably because of ego. If they'd let it go and it became a big hit, imagine how they'd look. It got put on a shelf, where it's still sitting today. I got a lot of cards and letters after the pilot aired, asking about it. But that's Hollywood. Too bad. It would have been a fun show.

So I had gone from being a moderately successful regional wrestler to being a popular, nationally recognized public figure. My work in commentating and movies gave me so much exposure that it allowed me to make the leap into celebrity status. I had branched out into many more directions since the days when I was just a wrestler, but I was no less obnoxious and outspoken. That reputation seems to follow me wherever I go. Barry Bloom tried to get my outspokenness in check a little. He warned me, "Jesse, don't tell everyone what you think of the role until you get it!"

My habit of speaking my mind was what

earned me the moniker Jesse "The Mouth." What seems to amaze people is that I actually make sense a lot of the time. Of course, I've always had my critics, too. But I'm thick-skinned. It doesn't bother me to have people yelling and screaming and picking at me. Throughout my wrestling years, that's what I was encouraging them to do! As I like to say in interviews, I'm loved by some, I'm hated by others, but what the hell — they all know who I am.

I might have gone a lot further in Hollywood if I had been willing to move there. At one point Arnold Schwarzenegger asked me when I was going to move out there and become one of the boys. I said, "Well, what about the schools?"

Arnold replied, "Don't worry about the schools. You put your kids in private school."

That's what stopped me. I thought, "I'm not living in a place where my kids have to go to private school." I'm not knocking private schools, but I believe that I owe it to my kids to let them grow up in a place where private school isn't required. They're only in school six or eight hours each day; they have to live in their neighborhood twenty-four hours a day. I didn't want them growing up in a neighborhood where anybody with the means had abandoned their public schools. A neighborhood is only as good as its residents' commitment to it. I know it hurt my film career, but so be it. My kids come first.

Again, fate: If I had moved to L.A., I probably never would have become governor. And after the election and what it did, with the long-range reverberations I see all across the country, I believe even more in that destiny.

CHAPTER 7

"THE MIND"

It wasn't something I planned. I'd never had any inkling of getting into politics. None. It had never crossed my mind. In a way, you could say that I didn't go into politics; politics came to me. It landed in my lap — or, to be more accurate, in my backyard. That made it impossible to ignore.

There's the Klingon in me again — that warrior ethic. A warrior is supposed to fight for the common good, to protect the community. In the situation that got me into politics, my community was clearly under attack. Even more infuriating, the attack was coming from the inside — from the elected officials who were supposed to be representing us. Their disregard of our wishes was like a slap in the face. Rest assured, when somebody slaps me in the face, I don't back down.

In 1990, Terry, Tyrel, Jade, and I were living in Brooklyn Park, an older, mostly developed neighborhood in the northern suburbs of Minneapolis. At the time, developers were coming into the area, looking to turn the few remaining potato fields into housing developments. This one particular developer came in and wanted to get the highest buck for what he was about to build, so he demanded that the neighborhood put in curbs, gutters, and storm sewers. We didn't need those things. We all had ditches to catch rain runoff, and none of us had a water problem. It was a waste of money to put those things in.

But for decades, Brooklyn Park's government had been in the hands of one of the greediest packs of good old boys the state had ever seen. Anything that brought them revenue, whether it was good for the people or not, they voted for. So naturally, these guys lived in the developers' back pockets. Anything the developers wanted, the mayor and his council simply handed them.

The citizens of Brooklyn Park were playing second fiddle to developers. Now remember, the developers put up their projects, and then they're gone; they're on to something else. The citizens live there year-round. So who do you think was paying for it all? Right. And who had the least say in how their money was spent? Exactly.

The council was gonna force this latest pile of gifts down our throats. They were going to give us these expensive curbs, gutters, and storm sewers we didn't want and make us pay for it with assessments. Worst of all, though, was where they planned to put the runoff water: They couldn't drain it off into the Mississippi because of pollution laws, so they decided to have it drain right into a local wetland nearby. This beautiful wetland, which bordered on Jewel Park, was about a block from my house. All that storm runoff being pumped in there would have completely destroyed it.

About 450 of us signed a petition stating that the proposed development was unacceptable. We told the council in no uncertain terms that we didn't want or need curbs, gutters, and storm sewers, and that we felt that they were doing it only to satisfy this developer. We took the petition up to city hall and presented it at a city-council meeting. We were voted down seven to nothing. That seemed a little strange to me. I could understand if they voted it down four to three, or even five to two. But the fact that the whole council seemed in such perfect alliance against the citizens seemed more than fishy.

I thought, "Wait a minute. Don't we elect these people to represent us, the populace? It don't seem like they're doing that." And so I started getting more involved and paying more attention. I started seeing that this core group of arrogant, self-centered old boys — Mayor Krautkremer and his cronies — was literally running the show. All you had to do was look at the council's voting record — it was 7–0, 7–0, 7–0 on every issue! They weren't even letting other people talk unless they agreed with them. They acted as though the will of the taxpayers was totally irrelevant. They were having their way with the people. Everything they said and did was to keep themselves in power and to keep everybody who didn't support them squeezed out. And we were paying their salaries!

I also found out that these same good old boys had used public funds to purchase a monstrous clubhouse, the size of a Scottish castle, adjacent to the public golf course — which they had also built. This posh, lavish place called the Edinburgh Club — which provided all the benefits of a private club — had been paid for with taxpayers' money!

So, the next time a council seat opened up, a group of us got together and decided we needed to get someone who spoke for the taxpayers onto the council. Joe Enge volunteered. Joe's platform was environmental: He was solidly behind protecting the wetland from developers. From the moment

Joe launched his campaign, all we heard was "You can't win on one issue!" Well, lo and behold, Joe won. So all the votes, instead of being solid 7–0, now came out 6–1, 6–1, 6–1 — except, of course, wherever Joe agreed with the council, which was rarely.

It was hard for Joe, though, because within the council you needed someone to second any motion you made — otherwise it never even went onto the floor. Joe would make a motion, and they would all just sit there! Nobody would second a motion he made, so nothing he did ever even went on the record.

I wasn't going to take that. I started attending more and more meetings and getting angrier and angrier. One day, I got angry enough that I went up to the podium and gave an impromptu speech about what I thought was wrong with the way Brooklyn Park was being managed. Then I looked at the twenty-year-incumbent mayor and said, "You're going to make me run, aren't you?"

He and his cronies laughed and said, "You could never win!"

Big mistake. I don't like to be told what I can't do. I walked out of city hall that night knowing that I was going to run for mayor. I figured it would work out all right: It was a part-time job and so wouldn't interfere with my broadcasting career. I knew I could do it. I was getting all revved up to start my campaign when I suddenly remembered that I wouldn't be around to do it — right about the time that the campaign would have to kick into high gear, I was scheduled to head out to L.A. to start shooting *Tag Team*!

No sooner had I gone out to L.A. to shoot, though, than the series was canceled. Suddenly, my schedule was free and clear again — just in time for me to throw my hat into the mayoral ring. The fact that the show got canceled when it did only strengthened my belief in fate. I believe I was destined to become the mayor of Brooklyn Park. And maybe, by fulfilling that destiny to become mayor, I sealed my destiny to become governor.

I hope I'm not destined to become president. I don't say that with arrogance — it's only that everything seemed to fall so easily into place in both of my other races. But I truly wanted to be mayor and governor — I don't want the presidency. I'll never say never, because you never know what will happen. But 99 percent of me says no.

My campaign for mayor was different, very casual. On most of my days on the campaign trail, I wore Zubaz (a brightly colored, baggy brand of pants made by a company in Minneapolis), a ball cap, and a T-shirt.

I learned quickly how underhanded the whole partisan system can be. It was a nonpartisan election, which means that no political parties were supposed to be involved. Yet leaders from the Democratic and Republican parties joined forces and cosigned a letter to all the citizens of Brooklyn Park. Their letter called the election the most important one in Brooklyn Park history and labeled me "the most dangerous man in the city." They urged the people, for their own safety, to vote for Krautkremer and not for me. All I did in Brooklyn Park was live there, pay my taxes, and send my kids to public school. Somehow that made me the most dangerous man in the city!

Well, to them, I was dangerous because I was a threat to their good-old-boy network. That was one of the reasons I later thought I had a shot as governor. If I could beat the parties when they were combined, I could certainly beat them when they were separate.

Ultimately, that was what led me to join the Reform Party. I began to realize how crooked party politics are. They're at each other's throats all the time, unless someone on the outside is threatening their turf. Then they join forces and tear the newcomer to pieces. Only this time, in Brooklyn Park, it didn't work — this particular newcomer was a lot tougher than they'd bargained for!

The problem I had with them wasn't that they opposed me; that's the American way — they had every right to do that. What troubled me was the fact that when the election was over, both parties, independently, came courting me. Now that I was in power, they wanted me to join them. That's when I realized that the end justifies the means with these guys. Why would they want "the most dangerous man in the city" to become part of their party? It showed me that they have no credibility.

We launched a very grassroots, plain-spoken kind of campaign. I don't think we spent more than two or three thousand dollars. We worked hard. The best way to win in a local election is to go out and knock on doors. So we did as much door knocking as we could. Something we were saying as we went around must have made sense, because as the campaign progressed we got so many new volunteers that we were able to distribute literature to every house in the entire city in one night.

We sent a letter to all the citizens of Brooklyn Park, introducing me and asking them to please take five minutes of their time to read what we had to say. The letter went on to describe the struggle we'd had over the wetlands, what the city was doing to us, and the fact that it wasn't listening to us. We explained that these were our elected people and that we didn't think they were doing the jobs that we elected them to do. We told the people how strongly we believed that with their help, this election could make a difference in the way Brooklyn Park was run. Our letter made an impact.

We also put up a lot of lawn signs, but for some reason they kept disappearing. On the weekends, I went out and baby-sat the signs. People would drive by a Ventura for Mayor sign, and before they'd have a chance to ask themselves "Who's Ventura?" by God, there he was — sitting right there in the grass next to his sign. I don't know to this day whether it was just pranksters who were taking them or whether it was a concerted effort, but we kept getting reports that certain cars were going around the city, stopping at our signs, and pulling them out. I wouldn't put it past that good-old-boy network to do a thing like that. They didn't care what it took to win.

My campaign manager was a brilliant retired schoolteacher named Floyd Anderson. He wrote a lot of my campaign literature.

One night, about a week before the election, I asked him, "Floyd, do you really think I can win?"

Floyd looked at me and smiled. "Jess, I don't think the question is are you going to win. I think the question is by how much are you going to win."

On election night we rallied at our headquarters, a little building in the woods, on land owned by the Izaak Walton League, about a half mile from my house. The building didn't even have a phone in it. Don Roggenbauer, a former ATF agent, was on a cell phone to Peg Snezrud, who was stationed at city hall. As each district reported in, Peg relayed the results to us. It became apparent very early in the evening that I was going to win, because as the first two or three precincts came in, I was winning at a rate of two to one.

I knew we had it in the bag when somebody came in and told me that people had been lined up around the block to vote. That's usually a good sign for a newcomer, a bad sign for the incumbent. If people come out in droves to vote, it isn't usually for the status quo. That's why the old-boy network — the ensconced Republicans and Democrats, the career politicians — don't like high voter turnouts. They're much happier if you stay home on Election Day!

Peg told us that a lot of the council members and their wives had gathered at city hall to watch the votes come in, and when it became apparent that I'd won, Council Member Bob Stromberg's wife broke down in tears and sobbed, "Oh, my God, what's going to happen now?" They acted like this was the biggest tragedy that could happen on the planet — the fact that the twenty-year incumbent was getting his butt kicked!

I won all twenty-four precincts, including the one Krautkremer lived in. I got 65 percent of the vote. Krautkremer, with a total of some twenty-five years in office, got just 35 percent. But the most remarkable thing about that election was that the people of Brooklyn Park, who were so apathetic in the previous election that Krautkremer had won with only 1,411 votes (his opponent got 1,100 votes), turned out in masses to vote in this election. Twenty-five hundred jumped to twenty thousand.

My mom and dad were there that night to see my victory. They were very proud. I'm so glad that they got to see me become mayor, because neither of them were here to see me become governor. My dad died three months after the mayoral election; my mom followed him a few years later.

The campaign and the victory were a kick, but the moment I heard that I won, I turned to Terry and said, "Oh, my God, now I gotta do this." But really, it didn't turn out to be all that hard. Once I got acclimated and figured out how the system worked, I did OK. My term was a four-year battle with the good old boys, which is what I expected. I knew they'd fight me on everything. Now that Joe Enge and I were there, all the council votes now started coming in 5–2, 5–2, 5–2. . . .

There was more than one can of worms that needed opening — I was looking at a whole pantryful. The first thing I did as mayor was to have the Edinburgh Club's books examined. They showed me a check register that was a complete travesty. Every fourth entry was blank — a check had been cut, but it didn't say for whom! These were sums of $800, even $2,000. I raised heck over it, and since I was the mayor the good old boys had to go along with it. I brought in Deloitte and Touche, one of the largest and most respected accounting firms in the nation. They went in there and came back with the report that the books were unauditable!

From there, we took our case to the Minnesota state auditor, Mark Dayton, a Democrat. He took a look at the books and said,

"Ah, we're not worried about it." Unauditable public records, with hundreds and thousands of dollars simply disappearing into a black hole, and he wasn't worried about it! That taught me that the good-old-boy network is so entrenched that one portion of government won't even investigate another. They all wash each other's backs. To this day, those books still haven't been audited.

It shouldn't have to be this way. Americans shouldn't have to work so hard to police their own elected officials. But that's the way it becomes whenever we get apathetic and stop making an effort to stay involved. Whenever we stop keeping an eye on them, we give the old boys a chance to dig themselves in.

How do they get away with it? No one questions them! No one takes the trouble to investigate! Politicians don't like to have to be accountable to the public. Look at the whole Clinton thing. Look how reluctant anybody is to say that none of this expensive legal rigmarole would have happened if Bill had just behaved himself!

I'm only speculating, but my suspicion is that the other career politicians in Washington all have skeletons in their closets, too. Remember what happened when Larry Flynt, from the private sector, offered a million dollars to anyone who would come forward and prove they'd had an affair with a member of Congress? They all have something to hide, so they protect each other. If that's not so, why wasn't there more congressional outrage when all this first came out? Look at all the people who went down because of Clinton. They were having affairs and doing the same thing! The only difference is that they hadn't gotten caught yet.

Not everybody starts out that way. A lot of good people go into the system with the best of intentions. But once you're absorbed into it, it's tough to swim against the stream. The current's very strong, and if you're going to swim against it, you have to be ready for a battle.

That's what I learned as mayor of Brooklyn Park. That's why we need to have term limits. We need to have private-sector people come in for a short time, do their job, then go back to their private lives. There can't be this tempting possibility of coasting along indefinitely in unaccountable luxury on taxpayers' dollars. It's too great a lure for too many people. The possibility shouldn't exist.

Because so few people bother to come out and vote in local elections, the good old boys have all the power in the world to entrench themselves, and once they're in there, they can have a field day with your tax dollars! If you think about it that way, isn't it worth a little bit of involvement and vigilance to make sure that you're not spending your hard-earned money providing posh lifestyles for a handful of entrenched officials? This is what happens when the citizens of a democracy don't stay involved in their government. Power corrupts!

A couple of weeks after I became mayor, I was at one of those public functions that mayors are required to attend. A man came up to me, introduced himself, and said, "Do you have any idea what you've done?"

I said, "I ran for mayor and won?"

He said, "You've beaten one of the most powerful old-boy networks in the state, and they don't like it." He was right. Over the next four years, they did everything they possibly could to disgrace me. Can you imagine what they're thinking now — not only did I survive all their petty little attempts to bring me down, but I went on to become their governor!

What do we have to do if we want to change things? We have to have the strength of our convictions. We have to be prepared to fight for them. And we have to be in the fight for the long haul. While I was mayor, I learned that government is a system of checks and balances — you can't simply walk in and change things. It takes time. I used to joke that it would have been nice if a magic wand came with the job, if I could just wave it and make things work the way they're supposed to. But unfortunately, it's not that easy. The bureaucracy is so huge that in a lot of situations all I can do is tell people the truth and let the chips fall where they may.

Government protects itself from the top down — state government is reluctant to get involved in local government, and so forth. And since the good old boys are ensconced from the top down, we have to be willing to whittle away at their network from the bottom up. That's the only way it's possible: in tiny local victories that eventually lead to bigger victories. The only way the system will ever change is if enough well-meaning private-sector people get involved in their local government for the right reasons and are able to resist getting absorbed into the political food chain.

The second thing I did as mayor was put all the council meetings on public television, over all the good old boys' objections. Exposure might create an educated, involved public, which isn't in the best interests of the old-boy network. The smaller the number of people involved, the more power the incumbents have. They can control it better.

The rules were changing. I held the mallet. I ran the meetings according to Robert's Rules of Order, and I now had the power to recognize Councilman Enge. He'd say, "Mr. Mayor, I'd like to make a motion."

I'd tell him, "Make your motion, Mr. Enge."

He'd make it; I'd second it. At least that way, it got on the record. Then we had to discuss the issue, and if the old boys were still determined to kill the motion, they'd have to vote us down — which they did, continually.

For the first time, the people of Brooklyn Park could see what the good old boys were doing, and they weren't happy! They were watching what we did in council meetings on the local cable station, and they could see that things weren't going fairly. It got to the point where we'd be debating a hot topic and people would jump in their cars, drive down to city hall, and storm in all red-faced to give the council a piece of their mind. It made a difference. In the next election, we found another person to run for the council.

We got that person in there. Then the votes were 4–3, 4–3, 4–3. . . .

Bit by bit, we were weakening the incumbents' stranglehold on the city. But the old boys weren't going to go quietly. About three years into my term, my mother began to get somewhat frail, so she came to live with us. But our house in Brooklyn Park wasn't really equipped to handle that many people. I knew I had to look for another house. I'll always put my family before any political life, because they're going to be around when politics is long gone from my life. Terry was big on finding a place where we could have our horses on our own land, because boarding is extremely expensive — you could pay a mortgage with it. So we bought a ranch in Maple Grove.

This was in the last half of the last year I was in office. In June, I announced that I would not be seeking reelection. In July, we bought the ranch. So at that point, we owned two houses. The good old boys saw this as an opportunity to disgrace me. They started whining that I should give up my position as mayor because I was no longer a resident of the city. It was ridiculous! There's no law that says you can't own two homes. The old boys hired a lawyer to try to find a way to oust me. By now, it was September. I had four months left in my term.

By law, the city was required to hire a lawyer on my behalf, because I was the mayor. I said, "That's ridiculous. I'm not spending taxpayers' money on something as absurd as this thing!" So I decided to represent myself. I knew I could do it. For one thing, I had right on my side. For another, I was the man who had successfully sued Vince McMahon!

The matter went in front of an administrative law judge. They presented their case; I presented mine. I enjoyed it thoroughly. Since I was my own lawyer, I got to cross-examine their witnesses. One day they put Bob Stromberg, one of the last remaining good old boys, on the stand. Believe it or not, in an attempt to build evidence for the case, Bob had actually been scoping out my house. He and a friend had been getting up at four in the morning to sit in the parking lot of Mama G's restaurant across from my house in Maple Grove, watching to see if anybody would leave.

I was doing morning talk radio at the time, and I left home at about four. I stayed at either house at the time, depending on what we were doing. My mom was in the new Maple Grove place, but we were essentially living in both houses, much as we're doing today with the governor's mansion.

Stromberg thought he had the goods on me because he observed my Porsche leaving the house at four o'clock in the morning. He was going to all this trouble to spy on me, all for the sake of this nonsense lawsuit!

My Porsche has tinted windows, and our house sits so far back from the road on a wooded lot that there was no way for them to actually see who was in the car when it drove out. So when I cross-examined Stromberg's friend, I asked him, "Did you actually see me get into the Porsche?"

"No."

"So you really don't know if I drove that Porsche out of the driveway, do you?" He had to answer no. "How did you feel about sitting in a parking lot spying on someone, waiting to see if a car would leave a driveway?" I asked.

"I have to admit, I felt pretty peculiar."

The registration for my cars, my driver's license, everything identifying me, still had my Brooklyn Park address on it. The judge ruled that all the law required me to do to retain my position as mayor was maintain a domicile within Brooklyn Park. In other words, so long as I intended to remain domiciled in Brooklyn Park to the end of my term, I was OK. The judge proclaimed,

"Since Mr. Ventura has announced that he is not seeking reelection, he has every right to look to his future, even to move his family out of the city." He ruled completely in my favor. Do you know how much of the taxpayers' money they spent trying to oust me? Thirty-three thousand dollars! People in love with power will go to any extreme to accomplish what they want.

My term as Brooklyn Park's mayor was my political boot camp. It was my first look at bureaucracy from the inside. I found out the hard way that whenever you take a stand on an issue, no matter how insignificant, people will line up around the block to kick your ass over it. By having an opinion, you make yourself a target. Why do you think Congress likes to hide behind closed doors at decision-making times? I learned that there will always be people who disagree with you, no matter what you do. And the more power you have over people, the more likely you are to have some little faction that conspires to trip you up, take you down, or strip you of that power. But I also learned that when you have the courage to stand up and tell it like it is, good people will come out of the woodwork to get behind you.

I'd always been in the habit of speaking my mind, and during my term as mayor I was able to sharpen my ability to separate common sense from bullshit. My involvement in Brooklyn Park politics exposed me to a broad variety of social and political issues and gave me the chance to sort out where I stood on them. I researched, investigated, listened, learned, and took stands. I owed that much to the people I was serving — I had a responsibility to be conversant with the issues.

While I was serving as mayor, my habit of speaking my mind and making sense got me noticed by a guy named Steve Conrad, who was the director of KSTP Talk Radio. And that's how I got started on another new career. One day, Conrad called me about an opening they had on the morning-drive slot. I had done a few radio shows for them, and they knew I was good on the mike and that my approach to political and social issues tended to stimulate a lot of debate. So I called Barry Bloom, we set it all up, and I hit the airwaves.

Talk radio and I were well matched. Cutting edge, controversial, "shock" talk is what gets ratings. I never really tried to be obnoxious or shocking, but I guess all you really have to do these days if you want to shock people is have an opinion. My opinions were strong; they were often different

246

from what was popular. But they were based on the truth. They were hard to argue with.

When my term as mayor came to an end, I didn't seek reelection because I would have had to give up my radio job. Equal-time laws wouldn't allow me to broadcast during a campaign unless my opponents got the same opportunity. Giving up my radio job for a $10,000 part-time job didn't make a lot of sense to me. Later, when I ran for governor, I had a similar problem.

After I had been on KSTP for about two years, they signed me to a new contract for another two years. I was just a few months into it when, seemingly out of the blue, they pulled me into the office and said, "We're gonna take the morning show in a whole new direction. You don't have to come in tomorrow."

I said, "OK." I went home and got Terry and said, "Load up the kids. We're goin' to the lake. We're on a long vacation — with pay."

She said, "What do you mean?"

I said, "They just fired me." I was on a two-year contract. They were the ones who took me off the air, so they had to pay me.

They were true to the agreement — for about five weeks. Then, suddenly, the checks stopped coming. I called my attorney, David Olsen, and said, "Where's my check?"

So David called KSTP, and Ginny Morris, my boss, said, "Well, we heard that Jesse Ventura refuses to work."

David said, "What are you talking about? You're the ones who took him off the air. He hasn't refused to work. Get him his check!" So she met with me, gave me my check, and told me that she wanted to use me as a substitute for other hosts whenever they called in sick or took the day off.

I said, "Uh-uh. That's not what I signed up to do. That's not what my contract says. I don't want to do that. That's unacceptable." We finally reached an agreement that I could live with. The financial part of the agreement is confidential, but I can tell you that I didn't have to work as a fill-in host.

So why did they let me go? KSTP's official line for public consumption was that I got fired because my ratings were low. But in this case the numbers don't lie. I was in the number-two ratings position with male audiences; David Brauer, the guy they replaced me with, was only number nine. That couldn't have been the reason. I never got an explanation. But I think one of the factors might have been that they got a little scared. They told me they wanted me out on the edge, they wanted me controversial, because that's what gets listeners. And I enjoy being controversial. It's fun; it makes for good radio. But being controversial can also get you an awful lot of negative attention, and you have to be willing to accept the negative along with the positive. I could handle it, but I guess they were afraid that any heat I took would also reflect onto them.

If I had to guess, I could trace their decision back to one specific incident. Our relationship was never the same after the day I used a particular word in reference to a state representative named Myron Orfield.

Myron is a true far-left Democrat. He's got a very socialistic view of government: Everyone works for the common good, you throw your money into a community pot, and the government redistributes it. I had Myron on the show one morning, and jokingly I said, "Myron, you little commie, you!"

Oh my God! I called him a communist! He must have thought I'd just trashed his reputation, because all of a sudden he was threatening to sue. The top brass at KSTP freaked. They thought I'd done something atrocious. One of the higher-ups even likened it to calling him a child molester. I took offense at that. I went ballistic: "What! I called him a communist! Communism is a form of government! I can go vote for a communist, if I want to, in every election. They're always on the ballot! They don't get a whole lot of votes, but they're there! I've never seen 'Joe Shit, the ragman child molester,' on the ballot before!"

The whole incident was incredibly stupid. Myron Orfield's oversensitivity — and KSTP's reaction to it — turned a molehill into a mountain. I felt betrayed because they left me dangling, feeling like I had done something wrong, when they were the ones who told me to be out on the edge, to be controversial and take risks!

But I did apologize to Myron the next day, on air. I realized I had mislabeled him. Do you know the difference between the definition of a communist and the definition of a socialist? Don't feel bad; most people don't. I looked it up in the dictionary. It turned out I was only half right. A communist is someone who believes that the government owns everything. There can be no private ownership. They redistribute the wealth evenly. A socialist believes there can be private ownership, but that government intervenes and redistributes the wealth. So I was only half right about Myron. He believes in the redistribution of wealth, but he also believes in private ownership. So when I apologized, I said, "You're right, Myron. I shouldn't have called you a communist. I should have called you a socialist." I don't think he took that any better!

From that point on, the relationship got progressively rockier between me and KSTP's powers that be. I said, "Look, you've got all these fancy lawyers on retainer here that you keep paying to do nothing but sit on their asses. At least I'm giving them something to do."

Terry told me to talk to David Olsen and Alan Eidsness, my two lawyers. I let a couple of months go by before I took her advice. But when I finally called them and told them what happened, they laughed! I said, "You mean I'm not liable?"

They said, "Myron Orfield's a public figure. You gave your opinion of him. They can't sue you — it'd get thrown out of court in a New York second!" Because he chooses to be a public figure by running for office, he's offering himself up for people's opinion, just as people are now free to state their opinions of me. They can even call me a communist now, if they really want to. He had no grounds to sue. And I wasn't even giving KSTP's opinion, I was giving Jesse Ventura's opinion! But from then on, the relationship got very strained over there. They got very standoffish with me, and I felt that they had left me flappin' in the breeze.

So for about a year, I was more or less unemployed. I did a little bit of work in Hollywood, but that was about it. Mentally, it's tough to be out of work. You start doubting yourself a little: What do you do? You're forty years old, no one's knocking on your door calling you to come out and be popular again.

Luckily, KFAN sports radio came along. They had looked into the situation, and they knew that KSTP wasn't telling the truth about my ratings. KFAN is very testosterone-driven radio. It's all sports. Their listener profile is about 92 percent men. They saw that my ratings among male listeners were great, and they thought I would make a good addition to their lineup.

On KFAN, my show took off. I'm the only sports-show host to have gotten a higher rating in the winter than in the fall. Fall is traditionally the strongest time for sports-talk radio, because it's football season. My show did so well that they were saying I'd brought the station to a whole new level.

My radio show, although it was basically sports oriented, took on a sharp political edge. In between discussing games, I railed at government overspending, I ragged on bloated bureaucracy, and I roasted corrupt government officials. The KFAN people liked to send me out to do shows outside the studio, because I did really well with a live audience. Every Friday they'd send me out to a family restaurant, and I'd do "Paycheck Friday." I'd say, "Let's see who the government took the most from this week," and I'd have people bring up their pay stubs.

At the time, I thought that with a solid mayoral term under my belt and a good, controversial radio show that was doing well in the ratings, I had gone as far into politics as I was going to go. If you had told me then that in less than two years I'd be living in the governor's mansion (at least part-time), I'd have laughed.

The idea of running for governor really sneaked up on me. Not long after I had won the mayoral election, another election came around, this time for a seat in the U.S. Senate. I started seeing signs around town for a guy named Dean Barkley. Barkley wasn't running as a Democrat or a Republican. He was running with what was at the time being called the Independence Party. I started looking into it, and I liked what they stood for. Like me, they were fed up with bipartisan mischief and wanted to put an end to it. They were big on term limits and campaign reform for the same reasons I was: Anything that kept the old boys' network from getting a hold on power meant that more power remained in the hands of the voters. I decided to join. The Independence Party later changed its name to the Reform Party.

I went to bat for Dean Barkley and became a huge supporter of his campaign. The fact that he was running for something as big as the Senate brought the party to a whole new level. Unfortunately, Dean didn't win, but he got over 5 percent of the vote in every county, which meant that he got the party qualified for the subsidy money that Minnesota makes available to major parties.

Dean ran for the Senate again later on. The second time around, I became the honorary chairperson of his campaign. But from the beginning of the campaign, Dean kept sidling up to me and whispering, "You know, Jesse. This campaign is great, but we have the wrong candidate. I think you should be running instead of me. You have the name. You can do it."

I said, "Dean, I don't wanna go to Washington; I wanna live in Minnesota; I don't wanna live out there inside the Beltway — who wants to do that?" I'm just not an East

Coast guy. I love the Midwest. It's my chosen place to live.

But at one point, around 1996, after I had left the mayoral office, I was with Dean in a parade in Annandale, Minnesota. I was there to show my support for Dean and his campaign, but the people were cheering me! And it was his hometown! Again, Dean said, "See! They want you! You should be running!" I said, "Uh-uh, Dean. I told you, I don't wanna go to Washington." Then as a joke, I said, "I'll tell you what. I'll run for governor." That was what started it.

It snowballed from there. All that summer of 1996, people kept urging me to do it. That's when I first started thinking about it seriously. There was this ripple of excitement going around town. The local Reform Party was solidly behind me. Since the parade, I had started testing the water a little bit, just to see what kind of public support there might be for my run. Most important of all, I talked about it on the radio and had gotten a sense from my listeners that they were overwhelmingly behind me. They'd call up and urge, "Run, Jesse, run! We'll back you. We're tired of these guys. Do it!" They put a lot of pressure on me to go for it.

Some time around August 1997, Dean Barkley and Doug Friedline, who later became my campaign manager, called a meeting with me and Terry in our barn on the ranch. They asked me, point-blank, to run. They were very solemn, very serious. I told them, "Look. Let me think about this for a few months. If I decide to do it, we'll announce it in January."

Terry was not exactly thrilled about this idea. She didn't want to see this happen. She tried to talk me out of it. But I kept telling her, "Look, honey, if I don't do this, who will? If we don't get someone in there soon, it's going to be the death of the Reform Party in Minnesota." I kept talking to her about it, until finally she gave in. I'm not sure how convinced she was, but she's always said I'm not an easy guy to say no to. I guess she's right. Look what she said twenty-four years ago when I asked her to marry me!

In January 1998, I went onto the steps of the capitol, called a press conference, and announced that I was running for governor. I went up there by myself; I didn't think it was appropriate to bring my family with me. I stood alone and announced my intentions.

Traditionally, candidates always come out surrounded by their families, to show how strong they are in family values, whatever those are. It's all bullshit. It's nothing but a photo op. I didn't want to use my family that way — just to prop up my image. The press said, "Where's your family?"

I said, "This has nothing to do with my family. This is business. This is the business of running the state." And a lot of people respected that, because it was the truth.

At first, nobody took my announcement seriously. Everybody thought it was a great joke: the big ex–pro wrestler running for governor — what's he gonna do, body-slam legislators when they get out of line? That first day I announced my candidacy, the press barely took notice. They reported it, but they probably thought it was just a publicity stunt. I think KFAN might have seen it that way, too. But I never did. When I made the decision to run for governor, I took it extremely seriously from the very beginning.

KFAN wasn't overly pleased when I decided to run for governor, because the show was doing phenomenally well. But I had stated that I was going to run, so I felt that I had to stick to it. It wasn't just my controversialism that made me popular, it was also the fact that I backed it up with credibility. People knew I had a reputation for standing by what I said. And I believed that if I lost my credibility, I would lose the very thing that was making me popular. I told all this to

Steve Woodbury, the station manager, and he agreed with me. But they still weren't crazy about losing me.

After the official announcement, Dean, Doug, and I outlined the strategy for the campaign. We knew that in a three-way race, we'd have to be polling in the mid-twenties by election time. If we could get that far, we knew we had a shot. We looked to see where Ross Perot had made it big in Minnesota during his presidential campaign, because we knew that area would be the heart of our movement. We found out that Anoka County supported Perot strongly, so we decided to focus our efforts there (and when the election results came in, sure enough, I got more votes in Anoka County than my opponents combined).

We targeted the areas that were strong on third parties — all in the highly populated middle belt of the state. In the rest of the state, we got what we could. We went up and visited the Iron Range a few times; that was Skip Humphrey's stronghold. We made some forays into the south, where Norm Coleman was big. But for the most part, we focused on the center of the state. And if you look at the election results, you can see that our campaign came together just the way we planned it: Humphrey won most of the north, Coleman got most of the south, and I got the Twin Cities and the suburbs, where the vast majority of Minnesota's population lives.

Then, too, we realized that high voter turnout would be on our side. Although Minnesota usually has one of the higher voter turnouts in the nation, still only about 50 percent of the population comes out to vote in nonpresidential elections. Well, to us that meant that one out of every two people on the street was a potential "customer" of ours. One out of every two doesn't vote! Why? Because they've been alienated by the two traditional parties, because they believe their votes don't count. We knew we had to do something to instill them with confidence in their votes again, we knew we had to tell them, "Come back and vote, and watch it count this time."

Democrats and Republicans don't like high voter turnouts. They like to have their dependable little core groups — a tiny percentage on the far left, a tiny percentage on the far right — who come out predictably every few years and get them reelected. It's which way the broad middle leans that determines who wins. Well, now they had a broad middle candidate, with access to the majority of Minnesotans.

We planned to saturate TV and radio with ads during the last two weeks of the campaign. Bill Hillsman designed our ads, and they were phenomenal. They were risky, cutting edge, innovative. Bill wrote our campaign song to the theme from the movie *Shaft*: "While the other guys were cashing government checks, he was in the navy getting dirty and wet." Bill had me pose as Rodin's *The Thinker* in one ad. In another, he had me as an action figure, battling Evil Special Interest Man. The action figure told Evil Special Interest Man, "I don't want your stupid money!" Bill's ads were so good that three of them went on to win national awards for political advertising.

Also, we knew that I could be very attractive to young people, who hadn't yet become part of the system at all. So we focused a lot of the campaign on them, urging them to take the opportunity to become part of the system, to make their voices heard. As it turned out, their response was greater than we could possibly have predicted. As Phil Madsen, my Internet guy, kept saying, "The election gods are smiling on you." So much of it went exactly as we planned it. The rest was just sheer luck.

My young supporters were the force behind JesseNet, the online network of supporters who kept each other informed of campaign news and developments. In fact, people are now studying the use of the Internet in my campaign to see what other applications it might have — the Internet had never been used that way before in a political campaign.

As spring turned to summer, I realized it was time to start looking for a running mate. The early polls said I was running four to one, men over women. So I realized it would be a good idea to bring some estrogen into the campaign to balance the testosterone. This is business; this is chess; this is war. You have to find your weaknesses and solidify them. It made sense to pick a woman as a running mate.

I also understood that education is extremely important to the vast majority of Minnesotans, so since I had no background to speak of in that area, I needed to pick an education expert. We sent out our feelers, and we found someone who was perfect: a sixty-four-year-old, award-winning elementary-school teacher and education advocate who carried herself with authority and dignity and had a straightforward, gentle, no-nonsense approach to education. Her name is Mae Schunk. I met her at Denny's over lemonade one day. She fit the bill perfectly.

She was a trouper through the whole campaign, an absolute pleasure. To this day we get along great, and we communicate well with each other. When I announced Mae to the press, they quickly dubbed us "The Body and the Teacher."

To tell you how remarkable she is, the very day after we won the election, she went back and taught her class! She called me that night and said, "Jesse, I'm going to have to resign from my teaching job. When do you think I should do it?"

I said, "Pretty quick! Like tomorrow? We've got to get over to the capitol!" That was the hardest thing for Mae, leaving her class. Politics is all new to her, but she's learning fast. And she's educating me on a lot of issues.

As summer wore on, I started appearing at as many public functions as I could: In every little town that had a parade, we were there, marching along and passing out literature. We were very grassroots. But as it got toward primary time in September, we realized we were in bad shape financially. Contributions were still barely trickling in. That's when the campaign got a huge, unexpected boost that literally put us on the map: the Minnesota State Fair.

The fair ran for the last week or so of

August, right before the primaries. All of us candidates had our booths. It was the first time in the campaign that I really got a sense that I had a chance to win. Coleman and Humphrey were on bullhorns, trying to drum up interest and draw people in. My booth was overrun with people. We passed out 43,000 pieces of literature. We went through almost 8,000 bumper stickers — we couldn't keep them in stock! We went through 6,000 buttons. People who bought our Ventura for Governor shirts were stopped a dozen times during the day by people asking where they got them.

On one of the last days of the fair, I ran into Norm Coleman. Jokingly, I said, "Hey, Norm! Look at my booth — I think I'm gonna win this one!"

He just shook his head. "Jesse, Jesse, Jesse. Rest assured, the winner of this election is going to be a Democrat or a Republican."

I just shrugged. "We'll see."

In spite of all this support, in spite of all the signs that were pointing to our victory, there was one major obstacle that still threatened to kill the campaign dead in its tracks: money.

Getting the campaign funded was another major battle we had to win. We knew that we'd need to raise at least $400,000 for the campaign, so we decided to see if we could qualify for Minnesota's Political Contribution Refund. To qualify for PCR money, your party has to have had at least 5 percent of the vote, and you have to have raised $25,000. We'd always had our 5 percent. The donation money we received at the state fair put us over the top of the $25,000 mark. But here's the catch: They don't release the PCR funds to you until December — after the election! So you have to find a way to bankroll the money until then. You have to get a loan.

You want to hear a great example of how the good-old-boy network protects itself? This PCR fund was probably created by some politician to make himself look good, probably in response to public outcry over how difficult it is to get a third-party candidate into a fair race. It was also created, so they say, to wean candidates off of special-interest and political-action-committee money, so that more people can get involved without having to sell out to PACs in order to raise the money to run. So the fact that this money is available made the politicians who created it look real good. But then they built all kinds of loopholes into it. They made it so that the money is almost impossible to use!

We were qualified for it. We just needed to get somebody to bankroll us until December, when the money would be released. So we went out loan shopping. Our first stop was Mr. Perot, since the Reform Party had given us their blessing. But for some reason, Perot didn't want to help us. When it came down to cold, hard cash, suddenly the party lost interest in me.

I couldn't understand. Earlier in the year, the party was all for me. They were even trying to get me to fly out to their convention in Atlanta. I didn't want to fly all the way to Atlanta at my own expense when I was in the middle of putting together a campaign! But when I told them that, they offered to fly me out themselves. They footed the bill for the whole trip! They were willing to do that, but when we needed money to actually make the campaign happen, they turned a deaf ear. I'll never understand that. I even had a private meeting with Ross Perot — you know he has the clout to set up that kind of loan! I told the party point-blank, "I can win this. The money's there; it's guaranteed! I just need you to back the loan." They did nothing to help us. Nothing. Zero.

It brought back memories of the time I'd tried to unionize the wrestlers — they were all for it as long as there was no risk to themselves. But as soon as the chips were down and somebody had to take a risk and make a stand, I was alone.

So we started going to banks around the state. We went to eighteen different banks, but none of them would loan us the money. Now how could that be? The repayment of the loan is guaranteed — it's already sitting there ready for disbursement, backed by the government. And still, somehow, that wasn't seen as a safe enough risk to these bankers. We even had an insurance company that was willing to insure the loan for $25,000. And we still couldn't get a bank to lend us the money.

I wonder why? Could it have anything to do with the fact that the head of the Republican Party in Minnesota is the head of one of the banks? I'm not saying that's what was behind it. But it's an interesting coincidence, isn't it?

Finally, we found tiny little Franklin Bank in inner-city Minneapolis, which was willing to loan us the money. They are in the business of making what are considered "high-risk" business loans to people of color, to help them start businesses. They have eighteen employees. Steve Minn, a Reform Party Minneapolis city council member, put us on to them. Franklin is one of the few banks in the state that isn't in either party's pocket. They said, "We don't even want your $25,000 insurance. We know you'll get more than 5 percent. We think it's a good loan."

What impressed them was that throughout the campaign, I never incurred a debt. That must have been my mom's influence sneaking in there — remember, I came from a household where there was never a car payment! We only spent money as it became available: when we got $2,000, we'd buy only $2,000 worth of bumper stickers.

We ended up raising $300,000 and getting $300,000 in PCR funds. All total, our campaign cost us no more than $600,000. On their campaigns, my opponents together spent over $13 million.

Franklin Bank made the loan to us three weeks before the election. Bill Hillsman was standing by to launch the new ads, and now that we had some money we saturated TV with them. The public loved them. They were up against Coleman's and Humphrey's stale, recycled, traditional ads, and they stood out like beacons.

I was the first third-party person to ever actually meet all the qualifications to use the PCR fund. Until this election, it had sat there untouched. Of course, now that a third-party candidate has managed to get hold of it and make it work, some Democrats and Republicans in the legislature think that the fund should be eliminated. I guess they didn't build in enough loopholes! Rest assured, if a plan to do away with the PCR fund lands on my desk, I'll veto it.

After we got the money squared away, my focus shifted to the debates. Now, I had gone to every debate, even before we all had our party conventions in June. Norm Coleman thought he was being smart by staying out of the debates until after the primaries. Coleman was the Republican wonder boy, the candidate who had left the Democratic Party to become a Republican. Well, don't forget that on the Democratic side, he had less of a chance to make a name for himself because he was up against the guys I'd dubbed "My Three Sons": Skip Humphrey, Ted Mondale, and Mike Freeman, all the sons of prominent Minnesota Democrats. As a Democrat, Coleman wouldn't have been able to get past that vanguard. The parties have become so entrenched that it's now become a legacy, you pass it down from father to son, just like a kingdom.

Now, the Republicans had agreed that whoever got the party nomination would be the one to appear in the debates before the primaries. But on the Democratic side, even though Mike Freeman got the nomination, all six Democratic candidates continued to debate. So Coleman figured it would be wise not to come to any of the debates while he was outnumbered six to one by Democrats. He didn't want them to gang up on him. So he stayed out of the debates and let me take on the six Democrats!

And they did gang up on me, to a certain extent. These six Democrats all thought, "Jesse — he's popular; he's entertainment; but he can't win." That's what the newspapers, TV, radio, and even the Republicans were saying. So while Coleman went into hiding, the Democrats planned to have a little fun with the colorful ex–wrestler and get a few good photo ops. They were pretty bewildered when they realized I could actually hold my own with them.

After I'd been debating the Democrats all summer, the primaries came along, and it shook down to Coleman as the Republican candidate, Humphrey as the Democratic candidate, and me as the Reform Party candidate.

And that's when Skip Humphrey made his major mistake, which in retrospect I think cost him the election. At that point all the pundits were saying that Humphrey was going to win, because as a fiscal conservative I was taking many of Coleman's votes. At that point, the Republicans were coming down hard on me, trying to get me to drop out of the race. They were saying, "You're going to get Skip Humphrey elected!" They tried to blame me instead of their own candidate! That's the nineties; you're not responsible for anything; blame someone else!

So Humphrey thought he was doing a prudent thing by making sure I'd be around to keep siphoning votes off of Coleman. Right after the primary, he announced that he would not debate unless I was included. It was the fair and honorable thing to do. But tactically, it was the biggest mistake he made.

After the very first debate among the three of us, in Brainerd, even the Minneapolis *Star Tribune* and the Saint Paul *Pioneer Press* said I won it. And right there, my momentum started to take off. Every three-way debate we had boosted my momentum that much more. Coleman and Humphrey fought with each other like Washington, D.C., partisan politicians, and I sat back like I was above it all; then, when I spoke, I talked directly to the people. I discussed the issues with them. I never used notes. I just spoke my mind. By comparison, Humphrey's and Coleman's responses sounded canned. Michael Braverman and Barry Bloom were watching the debates on C-SPAN, and they called me up and said, "My God! You're wasting these guys!"

This is where my opponents made the mistake of assuming. Even Coleman admitted, "I went with the total focus of beating Skip Humphrey. I never considered Jesse Ventura." They weren't prepared for me. They assumed.

It didn't hurt that I was in direct contrast to them physically. I'm a six-foot-four monstrosity. I towered over them. These guys were puny by comparison. I deliberately sat between them. I looked strong and powerful. Neither one of them looked powerful at all. I think your physical bearing plays a large part in leadership. People looked at me and saw a leader. As a general, or an admiral, or a governor, you have to carry yourself with dignity and power.

Coleman's big mistake was that he also believed the pundits who said that I would steal his votes from him, so at the end of every debate, he told the public that a vote for Jesse Ventura was a wasted vote. How arrogant! How pompous! To tell someone their vote is wasted! That if you vote for the candidate of your choice, your vote counts for nothing! I'd be willing to bet that a lot of the people who were on the fence between me and Coleman got fed up with Coleman because of that attitude.

After the third debate, the media and the public started rumbling that I was winning them all. My numbers had started skyrocketing. So do you know what Coleman and Humphrey did then? They both started canceling scheduled debates.

Now here's the interesting part: If Coleman or Humphrey canceled, the people who put on the debate would cancel the whole thing. But if I canceled, the debate still went on.

Thank God for the League of Women Voters. They sponsored three of our debates, and they said that they'd run the debates no matter who canceled. They even told me, "Jesse, if they both cancel, you can go on yourself." Humphrey finally killed his own campaign — by not showing up.

Humphrey had been portraying himself as the education candidate, saying that he was going to spend all this money on schools. Yet when we'd had a debate scheduled at the Mall of America with more than one hundred high-school kids from across the state, Humphrey and Coleman canceled.

And since the two candidates who "mattered" canceled, the whole debate got called off. That night, Humphrey went down to a Vikings game and sat in a private box.

About a week later, the three of us appeared at a debate at Blake High School in Minneapolis. That night, we were allowed to ask each of our opponents a question. When it got to be my turn, I turned to Skip Humphrey and, on statewide television, said, "Attorney General Humphrey, throughout your entire campaign, you've been stating that you're the education candidate and that young people and education are so important to you. Then I ask you, sir, why, a week ago, when we had a debate scheduled in front of a hundred high-school students from across the state of Minnesota, did you choose to cancel that debate, and instead go to a football game and sit in a luxury suite? Please explain to me why you made that decision."

He just stood there tripping over his own jaw. He looked like a deer caught in a pair of headlights. He managed to stammer out something about his scheduling and how he couldn't possibly do every debate that he's asked to do. But then why had he agreed to do it, if he wasn't going to show up?

Then I asked Coleman a question that

was almost as devastating to his campaign. Coleman had just been elected mayor of Saint Paul, and now in less than a year he was running for governor. At the time of the Blake debate, he had a bunch of ads running on TV to promote his gubernatorial campaign. I said to him, "Mr. Coleman, less than a year ago, I saw these same, identical TV ads running when you told the people of Saint Paul how badly you wanted to be their mayor. Now, you're running the same TV ads, only now you're telling us you want to be the governor. If that's so, then why did you run for mayor?"

I'm very proud that throughout all the debates I never used a single note. I never read a prewritten speech. I spoke from the heart. I answered the questions as I was asked them. I also did something in a couple of debates that was unheard of in politics. When I was asked a question that I didn't know the answer to, I looked out at the audience and said, "I don't know." But I also said, "If it's important, I'm a quick learner — I'll find out." The people saw honesty in me; in the other two candidates they saw political rhetoric, the same shit they'd been having shoved down their throats for years upon years.

The debates really got us rolling. With

each debate, the campaign gained a little more momentum. Even from the start, we never polled less than 10 percent. Now we were climbing into the twenties. Remember, strategically, I had to get into the mid-twenties to have a real shot at the election. Remarkably, when it came to Election Day, I was polling between 28 and 31 percent! By the time people came out to the polls, the press was calling it a three-way dead heat.

Our final big push came seventy-two hours before the election. We rented some RVs, set up a live Internet feed, and headed out on a thirty-four-stop trip around the state, straight through, no sleep. But I knew from my background that I could do it — it was less than half of Hell Week!

As those all-important last hours ticked down, we stole all the thunder from the other two campaigns. The press jumped on board with us, because we were having all the fun. We invited people, "Come along! Jump in your cars and come with us for as long as you want to go!" We had times when we were going down the highway with twenty-five cars tooting their horns, waving banners and flags. We came into cities in a whirlwind of noise. Later, people rushed home and jumped on the Internet to see if they could see pictures of themselves. There was running commentary, "Jesse's now left for Hutchinson. . . ." We literally stole all the publicity and all the momentum that weekend. That's when I started to believe we had a shot at winning. I always knew we had an outside chance, but that's the first time the possibility really began to seem real to me.

Even Terry started to feel it. She went on the seventy-two-hour blitz with us. It was her first real involvement in the campaign. I had told her from the start that I didn't expect her to be part of it unless she wanted to be. She could be as little or as much involved as she liked.

It was during that blitz that my confrontation with Hillary Clinton took place. It was on Saturday — I think we were in Rochester that morning — that Hillary had come into town to stump for Humphrey. One of the press guys came up to me and said, "Did you hear what Hillary Clinton said about you? She said it's time to end the carnival sideshow act that's going on here and get down to the business of electing Skip Humphrey. How do you feel about Hillary Clinton calling you a carnival sideshow act?"

I said, "It seems to me, rather than being

concerned about Minnesota politics, Hillary should be more concerned about leaving Bill home alone. He seems to get into a lot of mischief whenever she leaves him." You wanna start the fight, the Klingon's gonna draw the line in the sand. Strike us, and you make us stronger.

That was especially true of what happened to us when we got to Hibbing. Now, Mae Schunk and I are very strongly union: She's Teachers' Union, I'm Screen Actors Guild. But in spite of our pro-union positions, we couldn't get one single union endorsement. We had tons of supporters among rank-and-file union people, but none of the upper echelons were interested in us. The union officials were in the Democrats' back pocket.

We were on our way to speak at Hibbing Community College when the union goons showed up. When Mae and I started to walk into the auditorium, they formed a line across the entry to stop us. I walked up to the biggest one; I got up nose to nose with him, looked him straight in the eye, and said quietly, "I suggest you get out of the way." He stepped aside and let us in.

But the goons were so disruptive once we got inside that it was impossible for us to speak. They scared the students away and kept shouting us down. I shouted back, "Mae and I are vested union members. This is how you treat union brothers and sisters?"

But as we were getting back on our RV, they had the gall to say, "Jesse — if you win, don't forget about us up here on the Iron Range."

I told them, "Trust me. I won't forget."

There was one more incident that probably had nothing to do with any of this, but it did get us a lot of press. Just a little while before the election, a homemade pop-bottle "MacGyver" bomb exploded outside our campaign headquarters. In all likelihood, it was probably just some goofy kids pulling a prank, because two more went off in the surrounding neighborhood. Fortunately, no one was hurt. But the exposure it got us in the press didn't hurt our campaign, either!

When our seventy-two-hour junket was finally over, we came home and braced ourselves for Election Day. We'd covered more than fifteen hundred miles, and the whole trip had become a blur. Most of our campaigning had been by the seat of our pants. We didn't know what we were doing; we just made it up as we went along. We made mistakes, but we recovered beautifully. And above all, we were honest.

Election Day dawned. I woke up in the

morning, went out and voted, then came home, put the movie *JFK* into the VCR, and lay there in bed watching it, entranced by Oliver Stone's genius. I was done campaigning. Whatever happened next, I was satisfied that we'd given the good old boys a decent run for their money. I'd promised KFAN I'd come in the next day to talk about it, whatever happened.

As the day wore on toward evening, we got ready to go. We bundled into the Lexus and drove down to Canterbury Park, where we'd planned our election party. It's a racetrack — a place where long shots win. And since it was a horse-racing place, there were plenty of TV sets around.

On our way to the racetrack, we saw the moon come out. It gets dark early in Minnesota in November, so the moon was very bright. It had a broad, fuzzy ring around it, the kind it gets sometimes just before a snow. Just below the moon, we could see three or four shimmering ribbons of northern lights. We were all staring at that fuzzy moon with its gauzy skirt of northern lights when Ty said, very softly, "Dad, something strange is going to happen tonight."

Canterbury Park was like a coiled spring that night. There was so much energy in the air you could almost touch it. The way they had the place set up was great. There was a public part, then a private part, then a private private part.

Early in the evening, I got a call from Steve Woodbury, the station manager at KFAN. He said, "Jeez, Jesse. The polls are looking pretty good. Are you sure you're gonna be in to do the show tomorrow?"

I promised him, "I'll be there. It may only be for an hour, then I'd like to have the week off to recuperate a little. But I said I'd be there and I'll be there tomorrow, win, lose, or draw."

I was trying to stay very low-key, because I'm not a big believer in polls. I addressed the crowd very calmly. I told them that no matter what happened next, they'd done a great job, we'd accomplished a lot, and we had a lot to be proud of. We were full of joy, partying along with everyone else.

Then the polls started to close. In the initial poll just back at the primary, Humphrey was at 46 percent, Coleman was at 32, and I was at 10. The last poll before the election had Humphrey at about 34, Coleman at 32, and me at 28. The first precinct reported in, and it was just like the last poll. I turned to Terry and shrugged. "God. Maybe the polls are right. But even so, we at least gave 'em a helluva run."

When 2 percent had reported in, it stayed about the same. At 3 percent, I passed Coleman. I said, "My God — we're in second." I was beginning to think that everyone who said I was going to elect Humphrey by stealing from Coleman must have been right.

Then, at 5 percent, I took a 120-vote lead over Humphrey. It was Ventura, Humphrey, Coleman. At that point, in our hearts, we thought, "That's victory right there. Because even if we lose, we can say that at 5 percent we led!" Nobody gave us a chance — nobody, and for at least that brief time, we led.

Apparently, a few people knew something we didn't know. Captain Patrick Chase, the head of capitol security, was out at Canterbury Park with the Lincoln that was designated to drive the new governor-elect. Why was he there and not at one of the two big hotels where Coleman and Humphrey were having their parties?

He caught hell for it, too, from the outgoing governor, Arne Carlson, when he found out about it. I later asked Chase how he knew. He said, "I'd been talking to my troopers. The troopers are out there in the cafeterias among the people, and they said everything was comin' back Jesse. I knew you were gonna win."

So at 5 percent, when we took the lead, I went out and spoke to the crowd, and we cheered and hollered and congratulated each other again. Then 10 percent came in, and 15, and 20, and my lead kept widening. At one point, I was at 38, and Coleman and Humphrey were tied at 31.

When 40 percent of the vote had come in, Terry and I were in the private private room. I looked at her and said, "My God, honey. Can you believe it? We might win!" Terry didn't respond. As the evening wore on, she'd grown pale and quiet. My mother-in-law, Sharon, was rolling her eyes, going, "Oh my God!" It was almost surreal. I was very calm through it all; I didn't want to get overly excited, because the letdown would have been too much.

I called Steve Woodbury back and said, "Uh, Steve . . . I might be a little late for that show tomorrow. But I'll be there. And I'll be back on the air the following Monday." That following Monday never happened.

At five minutes to twelve, with about 60 percent of the vote in, I was at 37, Coleman was at 34, and Humphrey was at 28. The kids out in the public area were getting wild again. They were doing a mosh pit, passing bodies around overhead — I'm the only candidate in the world who's had three or four mosh pits going on at their election party! My people came in and said, "Jesse, the kids are getting wild again. You gotta go out there and talk to 'em, calm 'em down. They're gettin' brazen!"

I said, "No, I can't go out again, I can't. I've been out twice. I've gotta wait till the end now."

But they kept saying, "Jesse, you've got to go out there, it's getting too crazy!"

Finally, I stated, "Dammit! I'll go out one more time, but this is it. I'm not going out again until it's over."

Just as I stood up to go out, the three TVs we had on in the private room — one on each network — came up with a check mark next to my name. They were declaring me the new governor. The room exploded! Everybody went crazy!

I said, "Wait a minute! How can they do that? Four out of ten Minnesotans haven't been counted yet. If I go out now and declare myself the winner, and then it turns out I haven't won, I'm gonna look like an idiot."

Bill Hillsman came up to me then. He said, in his quiet way, "Jesse? You believed me about my ads, didn't you?" I said I had. "Then will you believe me on this?"

I said, "What?"

And he said, even quieter, "You're the

governor. Trust me. They know. They haven't been wrong since Dewey."

Then I walked out to the crowd. Modestly, I said, "Well, you're the ones calling me the governor. I'm pleased. But until I hear those calls from Humphrey and Coleman conceding the election to me, it's not official."

Forty-five minutes later, I got the calls from Humphrey and Coleman. They conceded and congratulated me. Then the moment I hung up the phone, there was Captain Chase and his security team encircling me. Protection for the new governor-elect had already gone into effect.

Amusingly enough, earlier in the night, Maria Shriver of *Dateline NBC* had told her national people, "I want to interview Jesse Ventura before the returns come in."

They'd said, "We're not spending our time on losers."

She said, "OK." Then she called me and asked for the exclusive if I won.

I said, "Sure, Maria. If I win, you can have the first interview."

Well, when I won, you should have seen those NBC guys scrambling. "We gotta get an interview with Jesse!"

Maria very calmly said, "I told you he was going to win. I've already got him."

They were going to take the assignment

away from Maria and give it to Tom Brokaw, but I said, "No, I agreed to go on with Maria Shriver. I'm goin' on with Maria or not at all." So she split it. She did the interview with me first, then threw me to Brokaw.

When you win, it's like an unstoppable force takes hold of you and drags you with it. You have to go where it's taking you. There's no way to stop it. It's a whirlwind, and you just ride it.

It's like boot camp. Once you get on that bus, and the bus pulls inside that fence, there's no way out. You're in the navy. Or, in a way, it's like being in prison. Having this job, in itself, is a little like prison, because you lose all your privacy. You become a prisoner in your own home. But I'll survive it. It's a pretty nice prison, as prisons go.

Once all the returns were in, we finally let go. We partied and laughed and cried and hugged. My friend Paul Allen, who had replaced me on the radio, came up to me and said, "Body" — that's what he calls me — "I've been to the Super Bowl. I've been to the Final Four. I've been to the Kentucky Derby. But never in my life have I experienced something like this. This is better than anything I've ever done." I thanked him, then I went looking for Terry.

She was curled up in her mother's lap,

crying, "This isn't happening . . . this isn't happening. . . ." She said, "I don't know how to do this! I don't know what they expect me to be."

Her mom said, "Just be yourself. That's all anyone can expect of you." She thought about that a minute. Then she dried her eyes and rose to the occasion.

I took her hand and led her to the waiting limo. It was close to three in the morning when they took me, Terry, and the kids to an inn near Canterbury Park. The troopers got us into our suite, told us they'd be right down the hall, and locked us in.

I had to get up at six the next morning to do *Good Morning America*. But there was one more bit of celebrating left to be done. Terry and I had brought along an old bottle of Dom Perignon we'd been saving. So when we were finally alone, we cracked the bottle open and poured each other a glass — the first in a long, long series of glasses; you just don't waste Dom Perignon! I was destined to greet my first full day as governor-elect with a hangover.

We looked into each other's eyes and smiled. She raised her glass and whispered, "My God! You're the governor!"

I smiled back at her tenderly. "And you're the first lady!"

CHAPTER 8

ACCEPTING THE SHACKLES

So I marched up this long, long flight of steps, and I pulled on a huge brassbound set of doors that even I had to exert some real muscle power to open. My footsteps rang against marble. There were corridors here, corridors there, massive staircases going up in two directions, vaulted hallways, columns of ocher-colored marble everywhere. In front of me was the rotunda, still prettied up in Christmas greenery.

Somewhere in this labyrinth — and I still didn't know exactly where — there was an office with a bronze plaque outside and Arne Carlson's name on it. I knew that in a few days, that plaque would come down, and another would go up. This one would have a different name on it: Governor Jesse Ventura. I was looking at the red and gold letters that spelled out quotes from George Washington, and at carved brass and bronze and gold leaf in the shapes of sheaves of wheat and ears of corn, symbols of Minnesota. I stared at these larger-than-life oil paintings of Minnesota's governors. And I imagined myself up there, in wraparound shades, tights, and a feather boa.

It's an awesome responsibility. I'm going to have to literally put my private life on hold, to a large extent, for the next four years. I'm under constant scrutiny by the people, by the press, and by security. From the moment capitol security came in and encircled me on election night, I've felt a little bit like a prisoner. I've never had this many restrictions in my life. I can't leave my home without my "protection." And even when I'm at home, there's security on duty, twenty-four hours a day. I had no idea how much it would change my life on a daily basis. They might not even allow me to rappel from the ceiling of Target Center during Timberwolves games anymore!

I've never really minded being in the limelight before, but since I became a political figure I've had moments when I've gotten fed up with the attention. One day I tried to get out for some much-needed R and R. I was out hunting for the day, in the middle of nowhere, and this one media guy still wouldn't leave me alone. At one point, he stuck a microphone in my face and said, "Mr. Ventura, what are you going to be hunting today?" I growled back, "Media people. You got a ten-second head start." It made the papers and the evening news.

People can do things to you when you're a public figure that they could never do to you when you were just a private citizen. I've heard there's a TV movie about me in the works — I have nothing to do with it and I'm not getting a dime for it. But somehow they can capitalize on the life I've worked hard to create, and tell my story without even talking to me about it, just because they can argue that I'm now part of history. You know what's even sadder? John Davis is the producer. He produced *Predator*. And Bruce Sallen is involved in it, too — he was in *Tag Team*. These two guys know me and have worked with me, and yet they're doing this to me. I'm very disappointed in them, that they would exploit my life to make a buck for themselves. And when I see them I'll tell them. Sallen's going bald; he recently got hair plugs put in. I sent a message to him: "You tell Sallen if I run into him, I'm gonna pull every plug out of his head."

If I had known the extent to which I was going to become a prisoner for these next four years, would I still have done it? Sure. It was a challenge. And I'll live through it. My family will live through it. We have it in pretty good perspective.

I've told you that I take my job as governor extremely seriously. But I'll tell you right now, it's only the second most important job I'll ever do. My very first day at the capitol, I made it clear to everyone that I'm not going to allow this job to interfere with my family. I make all my decisions based first on what is best for them. I told everyone that I'm not taking calls on Sundays — that's my day with Terry and the kids. I don't want to come home in four years to a house full of strangers. Besides, there haven't been any nuclear disasters in Minnesota. What could possibly come up that isn't going to be able to wait until Monday?

And of course, I have my detractors. There's no pleasing some people. Steve Sviggum, the speaker of the House, and Tim Pawlenty, the House majority leader, have given me the nickname "Robin Hood" because of my policy of "robbing" (as they're calling it) some of the proposed budget-surplus refund from the rich to give to the middle class.

I told them, "Well, if I'm Robin Hood, then I guess that makes you the Sheriff of Nottingham. If I remember the story correctly, Robin Hood was the hero; the sheriff was the villain." Hey, they do represent the wealthy landlord who's putting down the peasants!

These days, when you're in the public eye, the press does anything they can to try to bring you down. They take things out of context, they make mountains out of mole-hills. Now they're making a big deal out of the fact that I have a permit to carry a concealed weapon. So what? Why is that news? How does that affect any Minnesotan? That's been the lead story in the paper two or three times — the front page! Well if the governor can't have one, who can? If you don't trust your governor with a firearm, who do you trust? I'm the head of the state troopers. In fact, one of my state troopers said to me, "Why do you even need to have a permit to conceal and carry? You're our boss. It should go without saying!" And I'm highly qualified — I've had more training with firearms than all but a select few in the nation.

Because they insist on focusing on non-sense like this, the media's losing credibility with the public. The public doesn't believe them anymore. It's obvious that the press is working an agenda. Rather than dealing with things that affect the State of Minnesota, they would rather focus on personal things that affect me. And it's kind of funny, in a sad sort of way, that since nowadays the press tries so hard to get into your private life and expose you, that this is the best they could do with me. That's my big, dirty secret.

I don't get this. I just released a budget! This is what the state's going to be running on for the next two years — surely there's something in that budget that's worth discussing. Don't they think that's what they ought to be looking at instead of whether or not I can carry a firearm?

Recently, people have started telling me they want me back on the radio because they trust what I'm telling them. People keep coming up to me and saying, "Jesse, God, get back on the air! We wanna hear from you directly!" In response, we're getting ready to put together a radio show called "Lunch with the Governor," which will probably air on Fridays from about one to three in the afternoon.

They want to hear me telling them what's going on inside their government. I'm proud of Minnesotans for wanting to be that involved. They're an inspiration and an example to the rest of the nation.

I think the fact that Minnesotans are calling for this ought to send a message to the media. It's bigger than just them wanting to hear me. I think the people are beginning to feel betrayed by the press. They're seeing that the press misleads them, that it's not just presenting the facts anymore. They know it's going for shock, and they don't trust it to be accurate anymore.

Worst of all, they're not just going after me, they're trying to take Terry down, too. That's what really pisses me off. They should leave her alone. At one point Terry was telling the press that she was basically a low-profile kind of person. She said, "I don't want to be a big leader and have lots of power like Hillary Clinton."

The next day, somebody responded in a scathing editorial, "Rest assured, Mrs. Ventura, you're no Hillary Clinton."

Terry took offense at that. But I said, "Take that as a compliment — as the best compliment you could receive."

According to recent polls, I have the highest job-approval rating of any governor in Minnesota's history right now and the lowest disapproval rating, and I've only been in office a few months! And yet all the media can do is look for things to complain about. Sometimes I get the impression that the press sees someone doing really well, and they say to themselves, "OK, it's time to take this guy down."

It's bugged me that there's been so much discussion about whether or not I'm "up to the job." They kept asking whether I could do it. I told them, "I've jumped out of thirty-four airplanes. I've dived two hundred feet under the water. I've rappelled out of the hellholes of helicopters. I've done things that would make Skip Humphrey and Norm Coleman wet their pants. And you're questioning whether I have the integrity and the ability to do what they do? I'd say, do they have the ability to do what I've done? I don't think they do, either one of them." The media never questioned whether Humphrey could govern. They never questioned whether Coleman could govern, in spite of the fact that Coleman was only in public service for about the same amount of time as I was mayor of Brooklyn Park.

Every governor brings his or her own unique set of qualifications to the job. I'm basically an entertainer. Communication is my strong point. I'm not necessarily going to do this job the way a lawyer or an administrator would. One of the strengths I bring from my entertainment background is the ability to look at issues from a different perspective and to communicate a different point of view. That's where I can do the greatest good: observing and then relaying to the people what I see going on in their government.

My military training has really helped me gain the discipline this job requires. People worry about whether I'm going to get eaten alive by the political machine. If that was going to happen, I'd have been eaten already. I expect things to get rocky from time to time, but, as "Mother" Moy advised me, when things seem tough, I remind myself that being a SEAL was the best training in the world for the job. It keeps things in perspective: I've faced death; I've dealt with things that can kill me. Nothing I do will ever be as tough as what I did back then.

The structure I learned from the navy works well in this context. Although in everything else I've done up to this point I've been an independent person working only for myself and my family, I'm now part of something much larger. In the navy scheme of things, I've now become a commanding officer, and my job is to delegate and follow through.

The role of governor of Minnesota is bigger than I am. I understand that. That's why I'm willing to sometimes put on a suit and tie when I go to work instead of the jeans and T-shirt I'm most comfortable in. I get dressed up out of respect for the dignity of the office. I have to maintain a certain demeanor that's expected of the office. I have to swallow insults as the governor that I never would have swallowed just as Jesse. It's not what I do but what the governor does, and I'm fulfilling that role now.

I have perspective about it now, but I can't say that the transformation took place overnight. It's been very hard for me to get used to walking away from a fight. It goes against my nature. In fact, the day after the election, I made a comment that really got people stirred up. I'd had way too little sleep and way too much Dom Perignon the night before. In between all the official hand shaking I had to do that day, I managed to crawl into KFAN, clutching my head, and I did my show for an hour. During that hour, I indulged in one brief, small gloat-fest.

One day during the campaign, I had gone on the radio with Jason Lewis, a guy I used to work with at KSTP. He calls himself a Libertarian, but he's really a right-wing Republican; he carries the Republican agenda. Lewis calls himself "Minnesota's Mr. Right." Lewis and I have never really gotten along. When we were on the air that day, he had told me to my face that I couldn't win. He was so sure I'd lose that he wanted to bet money on it.

Well, when I went on the air the day after my victory, I couldn't resist a little poke at Jason Lewis. I said, "I wanna say something to another person at another radio station and I'm gonna call him Mr. Wrong. Mr. Wrong, who works in public television, taking from the public trough, Mr. Wrong, who said I couldn't get this done. Well, Mr. Wrong, you can stick it where the sun don't shine!"

After I said that, somebody (and to this day I don't know who) actually mailed Lewis a dead crow in a box, with a note that said, "Eat your crow, baby." The day it arrived in the mail, Lewis was out of town. In fact, he didn't come home until two or three days later, by which time that crow must have made a pretty pungent entree.

I was determined to start this term off on a fresh note. During the transition period I went out to all the heads of all the different government departments to meet them and find out what they do. A lot of them were totally astonished that a governor would come out and meet them. Some of these department heads had been there for twenty-some years and had never met a governor.

I worked hard for those three months, learning the ropes, introducing myself. The outpouring of enthusiasm I got from the people I met confirmed my belief that the next four years are going to make history. From Election Day on, the excitement kept building and building, to the point where I was really looking forward to the day after the inauguration, when I figured things would start to quiet down a little.

The inauguration was about the most formal thing I've ever gone through in my life, but it was beautiful. We stuck pretty much to tradition, out of respect for the office. Terry coordinated the whole thing, right down to the flowers and the outfits — one of those thankless, payless jobs that are expected of the first lady. She picked out flowers in Minnesota colors: blue delphiniums and yellow and white roses. We had a full orchestra and three choirs. Lunds supermarket donated thousands of blue and yellow sugar cookies in the shape of the state. There was even a team from Starbucks working the crowd — one lady with a stack of cups, another with a tank of coffee on her back and a nozzle in her hand.

On the morning of the inauguration, the temperature was thirteen below zero. There was a pretty fierce wind blowing, too, which brought the windchill down to about minus forty-five. In spite of the weather, we still drew a record crowd. I disappointed a lot of people, though, when I announced I wasn't going to rappel down the capitol dome as I'd promised — but if I'd done it that day, Minnesota would have ended up with an ice cube for a governor.

I decided that when it came time for my speech, I was just going to get up there and be myself. I'd made it all the way through the campaign without a single note. I figured that now was the time, if there ever was one, to speak from the heart.

But there was one note that I read during my speech — the one that arrived at my house the night before the inauguration. That note said, "I'm sure you must be nervous and apprehensive, maybe even a little frightened about that challenge ahead of you. But keep this in mind: you've been pushed, tried, and tested by the best. And you passed with flying colors. Keep that in mind . . . and don't change a thing. Sincerely, Master Chief Terry 'Mother' Moy."

We decided that a fancy black-tie inaugural ball for a select few just wasn't my style. We figured the inaugural festivities should be available to all Minnesotans. We held a huge blowout at Target Center, a 20,000-seat arena, about a week after the inauguration, and we made sure the tickets were priced within reach of the average working person — fifteen bucks each. And as huge as Target Center is, they still sold out. The place was packed. It was a blast.

Well, it turned out I was wrong about the excitement dying down after the inauguration. Barry Bloom told me that I was the most written-about person in the world for the month of January, except maybe for Clinton — and I bet he wasn't too pleased with a lot of his coverage. Even after all the festivities were over, it's just kept on building. What's happening here in Minnesota right now is incredibly exciting. People are smiling. Change is in the wind.

The most brilliant people are coming out of the woodwork to join my staff. There's a guy named Gerald Carlson, a fifty-five-year-old highly successful retiree from a company called Ecolab. He's set for life; he doesn't need to work. But he came out of retirement to be my commissioner of trade and economic development. Two weeks after he came on board, he came up and thanked me: "You've revitalized me. You've rejuvenated my life. I'm focused again, I'm not ready to retire, I'm ready to roar! My attitude is, there isn't one job we're gonna let out of Minnesota!"

I had no idea the kind of talent we'd be getting on board with us. One day I was getting to know the staff, so we were going around the room and each person was supposed to tell something about themselves that most people might not know about them. I told everyone I'd been the first swimmer in Minneapolis to break one minute in the hundred-yard butterfly. Then Michael O'Keefe, my director of human services, got up and said, "I have a degree in nuclear physics!" I almost tipped over in my chair. That's the kind of brilliant people who have come on board with me.

Something's happening here. Minnesotans are on the move; they're enthusiastic about their government again. This could be the start of the revolution we've been waiting for — if we choose to make it so.

But I can tell you right now, from what I've seen so far, we've got a big job ahead of us. When you're on the inside, looking at government on a statewide scale, you get a sense of just how huge the bureaucracy is. People think you can come into an office like this with a magic wand and right all the wrongs.

People come up to me continually with their personal problems — terrible, tragic problems — and I have great sympathy for them. But they don't understand that government is a huge, huge piece of machinery.

And if you look at government as an engine, maybe the governor is the carburetor. The pistons are the two legislative bodies. It takes all the parts to make it work. Nationally, Minnesota is third in government size, though we're somewhere around twentieth in population. This is one engine that needs a major overhaul, because somehow it's grown far too many extra parts.

I think many people come in like I did, with a clean slate and good intentions, then get gobbled up by the machine. I view the traditional two parties as in some ways very evil. They've become monsters that are out of control. They were created with good in mind, but they've grown into unhealthy things. The two parties don't have in mind what's best for Minnesota. The only things that are important to them are their own agendas and their pork. Government's become just a battle of strength, nothing more — a battle of power between the two parties, each trying to get the upper hand.

But now that Minnesota has a governor and a first lady who truly come from the private sector, a lot of light's going to be shed on how the system is unfair to people outside the two parties. A case in point: Between November 4 and January 4, I had to work twelve- and fourteen-hour days just to get acclimated and prepared for the job as governor. Do you know how much I got paid for the work I did during that time? Nothing! And this was on top of six months of no pay, since I had to leave my job at KFAN because of the equal-time laws.

That's one of the ways the system works against you if you come from the private sector. Now if Humphrey or Coleman had won, guaranteed, they'd have continued to bring in a paycheck, as attorney general and mayor respectively, during the whole transition period, just like they did during the campaign. But I guarantee you, they wouldn't have had time to do those jobs — not while working those long days with the transition teams. We need to change this. We need to see to it that incumbent public servants aren't getting paid for their jobs when they're not doing them.

I also see a real bias against the first lady in the way things are traditionally set up. During a governor's term, the first lady is required to run the residence. She's the head of the household staff, and she's responsible for all the official entertaining and functions that go on at the residence. She's expected to maintain an appropriate wardrobe — she can't entertain heads of state in Zubaz and a T-shirt. How much does she get paid to do all that? Not one penny.

Terry's a businesswoman. She has her own horse business at our ranch in Maple Grove. Since she's had these responsibilities at the governor's residence, she's had to hire people to run the ranch in her absence. That money's all out of pocket; she gets no compensation for that.

Now, if Mae Schunk becomes governor after me, do you think her husband, Bill, is going to quit his job as an executive to run the residence for free? Of course not. Or, if I were single, someone would have to have been hired and paid to do the job. But because Terry's my wife, she's expected to do this for free. That's sexism.

So during my term as governor, I'm going to work toward getting pay for the governor-elect during the transition period from November 4 to January 4. And I'm going to try to get it set up so that the first lady gets compensated for running the residence. It doesn't have to come out of taxpayers' money — the residence is maintained on private donations; she could be paid out of that. If I can get these things set up, they're not necessarily going to benefit me and Terry, but they will make things a little fairer for the next governor and first lady (or man!).

Nobody knows what to expect from the next four years. Roger Moe, Humphrey's running mate, even called my term a four-year blind date. A lot of the media has speculated that since I'm a third-party candidate, the legislature is going to degenerate into a three-ring circus. They're afraid we're going to get into a three-way deadlock on everything. I don't foresee that happening. We might get into a few two-way deadlocks, because it will really come down to which way the moderates swing — but that's pretty much the way it goes in bipartisan politics anyway. It'll be a two-way battle, but this time, whichever side has me will be the heavyweight!

It will all depend on who comes with the most centrist position — who's willing to move? My position has always been that since the two parties have gotten so extreme, there's nobody representing the middle. So that's where I've put myself to the greatest extent possible: in the middle, where I believe the majority of Minnesotans are. And see, it just doesn't make for a great insult. You can't hurt someone by calling them a centrist. It doesn't quite have that sting!

A case in point is the issue over the return of the budget surplus. I decided that since the middle class gets shafted so often in budgetary and tax matters, I was going to favor them with the budget-surplus return. It wouldn't even things out entirely, but maybe it would help a little. Well, here's the position I've put myself in: the far right-wingers are calling me a bleed-the-rich liberal, and the far left-wingers are yelling at me for sticking it to the poor! Their thinking is so entrenched in the extremes, they're so accustomed to thinking in terms of two parties, that they have to see me as one or the other. They can't fathom that I can take the best of each and be in the middle. They don't believe it can be done.

Right now, I'm being accused of being a Democrat a lot of the time because many of the Democrats are beginning to side with me. I think what really happened is that the Democrats saw the pasting they got in this election and were smart enough to move to a more centrist position, which is where I am. The Republicans are still hanging out on the far right, unmoving. So I'm now being accused of being a Democratic governor, which is ridiculous. I'm not a Democratic governor. I'm independent!

I'm thrilled that so many people came out to vote in this election. That tells me that Minnesotans have faith in our ability to change the status quo. We had the highest voter turnout in an off-year election in eighteen years — 61 percent! Now, 61 percent is good, but I bet we can do even better. Next election, I'm not going to settle for less than 70 percent.

So where are we going these next four years? Well, you know about the budget-surplus refund. That was the issue that made me run for governor in the first place — I couldn't understand how it's possible that we've had a $4 billion tax surplus in Minnesota, and yet my property taxes have kept going up by a steady $460 each year. I'm going to get that money returned to the people who paid it.

Education is my other big priority in the next four years. I truly believe that most of our social problems today can be tackled by better schooling and better parenting. Now as far as the parenting goes, I have to leave that up to the people — it's not government's job to interfere in how you raise your kids. But I can focus my attention on getting our public schools to do a better job of educating our young people. Mae Schunk and I have launched a plan to make sure that the money that was earmarked for classroom-size reduction is going to reach its intended target; rest assured, we will follow through.

Now that the budget's in for the next two years, my next big project is to do away with the bicameral legislature system. There's no need to have two bodies of legislature performing the exact same job. Minnesota has too many unnecessary layers of government. If we go to a unicameral legislature where everything is debated out in the open, we'll not only cut expenses, we'll make everyone more accountable. We'll eliminate the backroom conference committees where all the vote trading and political protection and power brokering goes on. Making the legislature unicameral would be more cost-effective and keep everyone more honest. It's worked for decades in Nebraska; we can make it work here.

I think the Democrats see themselves as government CEOs. They think it proves they're doing their job if they can show that there's been growth during their time in office. It's assumed (there's that word again) that any growth is good. But don't forget how *growth* is spelled for you and me: T-A-X-E-S.

I know my opponents made a lot of noise about tax cuts, and they liked to point to me and say that I didn't have a plan for cutting taxes. Now first of all, don't forget that when these guys talk to you about a tax cut, they're usually talking out of the other sides of their mouths about spending money. I figure a realistic goal for the time I'm in office is to keep taxation in check — if I can keep your taxes from going up, that in itself is a tax cut. I want the impact government has on people's lives to be minimal. Government should, ideally, do its job as invisibly as possible. If I do my job right, people will hardly notice that the government's been around for my four years.

So what will I do when my time as governor is over? I'll tell you when I get there. The job I have right now is gravely important, and it's so all-consuming that I have to concentrate on it exclusively; I don't have time to think about the future. I have to leave the possibility open, too, that Minnesotans will want me to be their governor for a second term. If they do, I'll give them another four years. I'm happy to serve eight years as governor, but I'll never do a day over eight, because I believe in term limits.

But don't look for me to make a run for the White House. I don't want that. I see what happens to everybody who takes that office: They all go in so virile and young, and then in the course of four years they age twenty. I can get by being governor, but being president would be too much stress, too much responsibility — I'd be the most powerful person in the world! I don't want that pressure. And I don't want to do that to Terry. I won't say *absolutely* not, but I wouldn't put any money on there ever being a Jesse "The Prez" Ventura.

I don't know if I'll do more movie work once my time as governor is over. There are still more roles I'd like to pursue. An all-time fantasy of mine is to act in a movie with Robert De Niro. But I might not do that at all.

There's a distinct possibility that once my time is up as governor, Jesse Ventura will disappear from the public eye forever. If I do two terms here, I'll be fifty-five when it's over. My governor's pension will kick in. If I retire then, I'll still have enough time and energy left to do a few things I've wanted to do all my life. My dad always used to say they had it backward: "They should let you retire when you're young and you can do all the things you want to do and put you to work when you're old, 'cause then it don't matter."

My dream of retirement is to sell everything I own, go to one of the Hawaiian Islands, buy a little cottage on the beach, and become the surf bum I pretended to be all those years. I'd spend my time surfing and marlin fishing. I think Terry would go for it as long as there was someplace where she could have a horse. I wouldn't even own a watch: I'd know that when the sun comes up, it's time to get out of bed; when the sun is overhead, it's time to eat lunch; and when it goes down, it's time to go to bed again. I'd grow my hair and beard out long so nobody would recognize me, then ride quietly off into the sunset.

It worked for Jim Morrison, didn't it? Sometimes I hear rumors that make me think the Lizard King didn't die, he just quietly, ingeniously slipped out of the public eye and is living on some tropical island even as we speak. That might be a poetic end to the public career of Jesse "The Body" Ventura.

But for now, I'm happy where I am. I took this on willingly, and I'll accept whatever comes from it. Whatever it takes to get the job done, I'll adapt. It can't be any harder than wallowing in the mud flats at Coronado, and I got through that. Besides, the food's a lot better here at the governor's mansion than anything they ever served me at BUD/S: rainbow trout with bacon and onions on top; filet mignon smothered in mushrooms, onions, and cheese; brandied bananas and cream, which just happens to go perfectly with stogies. Terry calls the guys who cook for us at the mansion the Evil Chefs, because they're always tempting us with incredible food. Just so you know, the Evil Chefs cook the meals, but I buy the groceries.

I'm willing to become a prisoner in my own home for a while because I have a vision for Minnesota's future. I can see a Minnesota that's even better than the one we have now, and I want that for our state. And I want to show the rest of the nation and the rest of the world what's possible when good people take a stand. If I accomplish that over the next four years, it will be worth all the loss of freedom and the lack of privacy I'm putting up with now.

I'm happy. I enjoy what I'm doing. I'm up for the challenge. I enjoy getting up and going to work every day. I even get to have some fun. Let me tell you about one of my first official proclamations as governor: When I heard that the Rolling Stones were coming to Minneapolis to play at Target Center, I declared February 15 Rolling Stones Day. It's completely official, on the books and everything, forever and ever amen. At the concert, I presented them with a gold-framed certificate full of lots of "whereases" and "therefores" and the seal of the State of Minnesota. The Stones loved it. And Minnesota will be observing Rolling Stones Day every February 15 even after I'm long gone. It's good to be the king!

CHAPTER 9

SELF-RELIANCE

I was in office hardly more than a month when I got booed and hissed by a bunch of college students for not spending more on education. I had just submitted the new budget. Do you know how much of the new spending in the budget went to education? Seventy percent! But that wasn't enough for them. They were yelling that they had kids to support and that they were trying to advance themselves by going to college. I asked them, "Well, why did you have children before you were ready to get serious about being able to support them? You make a mistake, you do something in the wrong order, you voluntarily make children you're not ready and able to support, and then you look to the government to pay for what you've done?"

Then somebody yelled, "But my husband ran off!"

I said, "Is that my fault? That you got involved with a jerk?" And they booed me!

Now, I'm not saying all young people are like this. In fact, that same day, other college kids who heard that whole exchange sent me notes apologizing for the ones that booed me. But it just goes to show you the attitude of entitlement that's very prevalent in this country right now.

This is the kind of thinking you get when young people start doing grown-up activities before they have a grown-up level of maturity. That's why I think socialism becomes appealing to some young people. They move out of that carefree period of their lives, they get a family and responsibilities, and then they start to get worried. Up until now, their parents have been taking care of them, and they don't yet have a good sense of what it means to take care of themselves. So they start looking around for someone else who's going to take care of them. That's when they turn to the government. That's one handy way you could define socialism: It's federalized mommy and daddy.

College has always been the bastion of socialism. It's the birthplace of new ideas, and that's good. But it's fun to get to be my age and have watched the college kids protest and demand more money; fifteen years later, after they've had jobs, they look at half their paychecks going to the government and my, how their ideas change! All of a sudden, they see these great social ideas in a different light. They've been footing the bill for a few years!

But it doesn't have to be this way. If we took more responsibility for teaching young folks the value of self-reliance, the thought of looking to the government to solve all their problems wouldn't even cross their minds. A few generations ago, we were all raised that way: You stand on your own two feet; if you get yourself into trouble, you get yourself out of it. Somehow over the last few decades, that message has gone missing from what's being passed down from one generation to the next. It's a dangerous trend.

Believe me, our government as it is now is not something you want to rely on for your own personal security. It doesn't have your best interests at heart. But even if it did — and it should — a democratic government should never be relegated to the role of full-time, cradle-to-grave caretaker. And that goes doubly so for anyone who is actually capable of taking care of themselves.

Over the past few decades, we've gotten into a bad habit of looking to the government to solve every personal and social crisis that comes along. People have really come to misunderstand government's scope. There's only so much it can do. For one thing, it's a terrible social regulator. And morals and values aren't things that legislation can even touch. You can't legislate morality. It doesn't work.

There are other ways to handle those things, better ways. One is called parenting. The other is called community. I was very fortunate: I was raised in a time and place where family and community were still very strong, when people fought to keep family and community together and keep them respectable. If you got out of line, you had an army of family, friends, and neighbors who you knew would be personally disappointed in you — people you cared about and respected. Have you ever felt what it's like to know you've disappointed someone you cared about, someone who really knew you and knew you were capable of much better behavior? That's a far more effective means of "regulation" than anything government can do to you. And it doesn't even raise your taxes!

A democratic government's only role is to help keep the playing field level for its citizens and to do for people what they truly cannot do for themselves. The government's role is not to guarantee jobs or wages or to dole out money to anyone who asks for it. Once we start expecting government to take on those roles, we're not going to like the consequences we have to live with. We can't afford to think of government as a bottomless well of money. Remember, government doesn't make a penny. The only money government has comes from working people: you and me. If we expect government to be ready at our beck and call, then we'd better be prepared to hand over more and more of our paychecks in taxes. Somebody's got to pay for it all!

It's not supposed to be that way. Not in this country. I find it totally unacceptable to pay almost half of my income to government. When that happens, rest assured, government has grown far beyond the job the Constitution created it to do.

It's a vicious circle. The more we rely on government to solve our problems, the bigger and more expensive it becomes. The bigger and more expensive our government becomes, the more of our paychecks it takes and the more of our personal decisions it starts taking over from us. And the more money and decision-making power we lose, the more we lose our freedom. That's why it's so important for us to keep our government in check. Remember that old saying: "If they have to do it for you, they're gonna do it to you."

Freedom isn't just something that's handed to you. It can't be. Simply by its nature, freedom requires independence. How free can you be, really, if you're looking to someone else to provide for your needs? If someone's providing for you, then they're also making decisions for you. How free is that? True freedom means you stand on your own, sink or swim. You have to be able to make sound decisions and live with the consequences if you're truly going to be free. In this country, more than any other in the world, we have a tremendous opportunity for freedom. But until we accept the responsibility that's part and parcel of freedom, we'll never truly have it. There is no real freedom without self-reliance.

Self-reliance is going to take time. People have become so accustomed to leaning on the government for help. Our dependence on government didn't happen overnight; it's not going to go away overnight. It's probably going to take a generation or two.

There's no magic for it. It's just a matter of not looking to government to correct our mistakes. I have all the sympathy in the world for single parents. And I do think that the government should step in when one parent runs off and doesn't support the kids. Absolutely. But the line has to be drawn somewhere. Certainly, accidents happen, and as a just society we should have a safety net for the victims of accidents. But I'm making a distinction here between these cases, which are legitimate need, and the attitude I'm seeing in many young people today. How fair is it, how mature is it, to sit there and blame the government for not supporting their rotten choices?

Now, it's certainly government's responsibility to go after these creeps and throw their asses in jail or garnish their wages if they don't take responsibility for the kids they created. We should make life miserable for them. This is the kind of thing I'm talking about when I say that government should be there to provide a safety net for the things you as an individual can't do on your own.

But anything you can do on your own, even if it's difficult, even if it requires a few sacrifices, you should tighten your belt and take responsibility for. You have no right to take other people's money for something you can do on your own. It's not fair to the rest of us.

Take going to college, for example. Nobody says you have to graduate in four years. You can go to college for however long it takes. And these days, bright high-school kids can take college courses for free. They can actually get college credit for stuff in high school. They can have half their credits done by the time they get to college! Where there's a will, there's a way. I think we're a stronger nation if we're made up of strong-willed, self-reliant people. Conversely, the more dependent and apathetic and weak-willed we become, the weaker a nation we'll be. That's the trend I'm seeing, and it scares me.

Politicians have started catering to this "I'm entitled" mentality. Believe it or not, in this election, Skip Humphrey and Roger Moe were promising two years of free college to every young Minnesotan. Imagine what that would have done to the budget. Imagine what our taxes would have looked like if we'd have had to foot the bill for that. We'd be hamstringing ourselves — and our own kids — with enormously high taxes for a lifetime, just so that for two years some kids could coast through college on free tuition. How shortsighted is that? And who truly appreciates anything they don't have to work for?

We're fooling ourselves if we think that everybody who goes to college is committed to getting a four-year degree. I kept saying, "Skip, if you're going to give them two years of free college, at least make it the last two, so that somewhere along the line they had to earn it!" My God, if Humphrey and Moe had had their way, we'd be reenacting the movie *Animal House* on a statewide scale. An associates degree would become nothing more than graduating from fourteenth grade.

Besides, you know they never would have gotten that plan through the legislature. It was a typically empty partisan promise. Humphrey and Moe really thought that young people were stupid enough to believe them. Fortunately, the young people saw right through that one. They voted for me.

I'm all for loving your fellow man, but we should expect him to love back. It's selfish for someone to sit back and think they deserve the fruits of someone else's labor. That's what we're doing any time we expect government to pay for something. Where do you think government gets its money? We should demand that people do whatever work they're capable of — however humble it might be — and if necessary, we can make up the difference. I think if taxpayers saw that people were making an honest effort to contribute something, it would make it easier to help them the rest of the way. Welfare should be a safety net, not a lifestyle.

But we've let it get to the point that if someone is on welfare and they get a job, they get penalized! It should be the other way around. That's the mind-set we have to change.

That's what I want to tell this new generation: Take responsibility for your actions. If you make a bad choice, by God pull up your bootstraps and live with it. When you go through life accepting responsibility and working through the tough times, you develop a solid, reliable core inside yourself that's called character. And it will make you a better person in everything you do.

I believe that deep down, people want to be self-reliant. I think young people, if given a chance, will jump at independence. If they're raised with a sense of personal responsibility and a belief in their own abilities, they'll step forward and take charge of their own lives. It's up to us to give them that chance.

I truly believe that the most remarkable phenomenon in this election was the young people who came forward and got involved in the political system for the first time. We have to recognize the significance of that: We have a whole new generation here that is telling us that if we make room for them and give them a chance to be heard, they have something to say! Whatever we do from here, we have to make sure that this new generation is heard and that we do whatever it takes to keep them involved. They're our future.

Recently, I had a chance to speak to the students at Roosevelt High School, where I graduated in 1969. I told them the same thing I want to tell all of America's young people: Be independent. You can depend on yourself. The American dream is still there. You can still work hard for your dream and achieve it. Live your dreams. Because without dreams, life becomes very stagnant. It doesn't matter what your dreams are — one person's dream might be insignificant to someone else, but that's unimportant. I'm living proof that dreams can come true: I sat in that same chair, right in that same school. I'm no more special than anyone else. And if I can become governor, so can you. Go after your dreams!

CHAPTER 10

LOOKING NATIONAL

I'm in this to do as much as I can to affect the big picture. I can envision changes in attitudes and policies that would make our country great again, and while I have all this attention focused on me, I'm going to speak my mind. Then I'll back up what I say with action. In many ways, what happens in Minnesota within the next four years will be a proving ground for what can happen nationally. If we can make these changes work here, we will boost people's confidence that they can work nationwide. The excitement that this election has generated reaches far beyond the borders of Minnesota. People all across the nation are energized by the hope of change. People want to get their faith in the American dream back again.

Far too much of our society and our lives today are influenced by the media and by politicians with extreme agendas. How did the media and the extremists get so much power? Because people are afraid of them and because they've got seniority. They've become entrenched. In so much that I've seen of the way government works, whoever's been there the longest carries the biggest switch. People in public office have to renew themselves. If the same people keep carrying the power, they develop into a good-old-boy network, just like the one we had in Brooklyn Park.

Our country is at a crossroads right now. Change is in the wind. I think the events that have just happened in Washington are causing everyone to take a long, hard look at what our government's become. And now is the time to do something about it — now that we have it all out in the light.

We need to bring back a little honesty and integrity to our government. We can do that, but only if we're willing to stop making popularity so important. The right answer is not always the popular one, at least initially. You have to have a vision for further down the line. That's where integrity comes in. We need people who will say what they believe and why, and who will stick by what they say until they make it happen.

One time when I was mayor of Brooklyn Park, I was out visiting Washington, D.C., and an old politician took me aside and said, "You're that young new mayor from Minnesota, aren't you? Can I give you a little piece of advice? Always vote like you're not gonna seek reelection. That way you never compromise your integrity."

I've always tried to maintain that position. I don't make decisions based on whether Jesse Ventura's gonna get reelected in four years. In fact, if I do seek reelection, my whole campaign is going to be very simple: If you think I did a good job and you want me to stay in for four more years, vote me in; if you think someone else can do a better job, vote him or her in.

We pay way too much of our income to the government. I want to see income tax done away with entirely. Income tax could be replaced with a 15 percent across-the-board sales tax. People are studying this right now, and there's plenty of good evidence to indicate that it could work. But it would have to be done nationally — that's the only way it could work. After it's in place nationally, then each individual state could add its own taxes on top of that.

I'm totally sold on this idea. We'd be able to take home the gross on our paychecks! We'd be in control of how much tax we paid by choosing how much to buy. We wouldn't be penalized anymore for working hard and saving money! And it would be much fairer, because in the current system there are plenty of industries (legal and illegal) that get away with paying no taxes — gambling, drug dealers, cottage industries. But since everybody has to buy things, the tax would cover everyone, even illegal immigrants. But it's got to start with the feds. And it will only happen if we, the citizens, show a lot of support for it.

I want to make government more directly accountable to the people. Nothing we're paying people in public office to do should be going on behind closed doors. We have to do whatever is necessary to eliminate backroom politics and under-the-table wheeling and dealing. We need to create a climate in government where openness and honesty have chances to flourish.

In order to keep government healthy, we have to have a lot of turnover. We have to have term limits. We can't allow people to get ensconced. Our government was founded with the idea that it would be butchers, bakers, and candlestick makers going into office and serving; then, when their terms were done, they'd go back to their trades. Jefferson and the other founding fathers never had the idea that people were going to make thirty-year careers out of politics. That was never the intention. Americans need fresh ideas and constant turnover, otherwise the machine becomes a monster.

And most important of all, we need to be involved, every single one of us. Our government will never truly be a government by, of, and for the people if people are too apathetic to do their parts. Voting is a privilege, but it's also a responsibility. People have given their lives to protect our right to vote. We owe it to ourselves and to each other to exercise that right.

In a sense, even if you don't vote, you vote by default. A vote not used is implied consent. You're volunteering for taxation without representation. They can do whatever they want to you because you haven't challenged them.

Why do we stand for it? On Election Day, your opinion matters just exactly as much as anyone else's. With your vote, you have a chance to make yourself heard. It's yours. Don't throw it away! I'll never understand why people whine and complain about the state their government's in, then they throw away the one civil action they can perform to change things. It pisses me off when I hear people say, "Yeah, but I only have one vote. What's one vote gonna do?" Well, for God's sake, how many votes do you think anyone else has?

You don't believe in the power of your

vote? Well, take a look at what happened in Minnesota on November 3, 1998. Minnesotans didn't have any more votes per person than anyone else, yet with the power of our votes, we changed the course of history. Everybody said a third party could never win. They even said people who voted for me were wasting their votes. Well, look at what all those "wasted" votes accomplished. People just like you, who had been convinced that their vote didn't matter, came out to the polls and made their votes count. What do you think would have happened if Minnesotans had stayed away at this last election?

Change starts at the grassroots level, and that's where we need to focus our efforts. No election is too small. I'm urging you: Go out and get involved in local politics. Go to schoolboard meetings. Check up on your town council. Make them accountable. Make sure they're representing you. That's what you're paying them to do, isn't it? You'll be amazed at the difference your involvement can make.

And we need to send a message to our young people: We have expectations of you. Take responsibility for your own actions. It might be tough in the short run, but in the long run, you'll respect yourself more for it, and your community will be proud of you.

We really can't blame young people entirely for their apathy. Government today is so full of contradictions and hypocrisy that it can't be taken seriously. A case in point: We don't send a clear message to young people about when we expect them to be legally responsible for their choices. We can send them off to die in a war at age eighteen, but we won't even let them go into a bar and order a beer until they're twenty-one. If the government enforces these kinds of nonsensical contradictions, then of course people are going to lose faith in it. We need a single, nationwide age of adulthood, so that there's no ambiguity.

These are the changes I want to see our country make. They're mostly changes in attitude. We must become, as a nation, more honest, open, and self-reliant. And we must expect no less of our government.

The Reform Party has a huge amount of potential to spearhead these changes. Its philosophy is outstanding: Reform Party members believe in term limits, campaign reform, a ban on PAC contributions, openness, accountability — many of the principles that will keep our government honest. The rules are easy to keep because they basically keep you clean; they keep you from becoming corrupt. But the Reform Party needs to reinvent itself a bit. They could have been a major national party if Ross Perot hadn't faltered. But now that he has, he needs to step down and let someone else take the reins. If the party doesn't get some fresh blood, it's going to become anemic and die.

Nothing personal against Perot — I think he's commendable. I voted for him twice. But for whatever reason, he wants to remain out front. When you call the party headquarters in Dallas, they still answer the phone, "Perot in ninety-six." He's fallen a great distance from the first time he ran, and he fell again the second time. He had better step aside in this next election or the party won't exist nationally anymore.

We need a strong presidential candidate for the Reform Party in this next election. It's extremely important to the survival of the party. The party's got its feelers out right now. There are plenty of powerful candidates out there who could do it.

If we can get someone with major name recognition to step forward, it can work. A lot of people in the party are telling me I'm the man, that I have all the power. But I don't want that power. I'm happy doing what I'm doing. Once they come up with a good candidate, I'll support the person they pick.

The time is right, in this upcoming election, for a strong reform candidate to step forward. I mean, think about it — who else have we got? Al Gore? He's about as exciting as watching paint dry. Nothing personal, but I don't see Al Gore stimulating the masses.

And the Republicans are just going to shoot themselves in the feet again, coming in with that far-right agenda. Americans don't want the government telling them how to live their lives. Their candidate's never gonna fly as long as they stick to the extreme agenda that's currently driving the Republican Party. That's why Norm Coleman didn't make it. He had to sell out to the far right-wingers, then he later tried to come back to a centrist position. All through the debates you'd hear him say, "Well, I agree with Jesse." Both he and Humphrey said that, actually. But in the eyes of the voters it was too late. They'd already established themselves on the extremes. And trying to swing away from their stated positions just made them look like they lacked integrity. The people are on to these political tricks, and they're tired of it.

Do you want to know who I have my eye on? And from what I'm told, a lot of other

Reform Party people are watching him too. Colin Powell. He could do it. He has that leadership quality. He makes sense when he speaks, and he speaks with integrity. He'd break a barrier, being the first black to become president. He'd be refreshing. If he volunteered, I'd be right there to jump on board with him. A person like him could truly put the third party on the map for the nation, as I've done for Minnesota. If he ran and won, the third party would be here forever and ever, amen.

Americans are famous the world over for being pioneers and visionaries. We can be those things again. We're still the most powerful country in the world; certainly, we're the wealthiest. If we stop focusing on popularity and polls and media spin and look to our hearts and souls for the answers, if we're willing to have the courage to accept responsibility and stand by our convictions, we can be a great nation again.

We're a beacon to the world, an example of what people can accomplish when they truly live in freedom. It's ours to embrace. If we embrace it, we won't lose it. To all Americans who have lost faith in the American dream, I'm living proof that it's still alive and well. It's still our nation — we can still make it what we want it to be. And to all the young people who have voluntarily come out to take part in the system, welcome. Welcome to democracy in the making. May your visions of the future inspire all our lives.

The employees of Thorndike Press hope you have enjoyed this Large Print book. All our Large Print titles are designed for easy reading, and all our books are made to last. Other Thorndike Press Large Print books are available at your library, through selected bookstores, or directly from us.

For information about titles, please call:

(800) 257-5157

To share your comments, please write:

Publisher
Thorndike Press
P.O. Box 159
Thorndike, Maine 04986